IN THE SAME ORIGINAL FORMAT, GENERAL EDITOR AND DESIGNER DAVID BROWER

BY THE SAME AUTHOR

I will not conceal his parts, nor his power,
nor his comely proportion. . . .
He maketh the deep to boil like a pot:
he maketh the sea like a pot of ointment.
He maketh a path to shine after him; one would
think the deep to be hoary.
Upon the earth there is not his like, who
is made without fear.
He beholdeth all high things:
he is king over all the children of pride.
                          Job 41 (of leviathan)

Wake of the Whale

The great flank slid by him as dark and graffitoed as a subway pulling away from 125th Street. Bill, mildly buffeted but unharmed, was the commuter who had missed the train. As the flank passed, he saw the scratches, the scars, the patterns of new and old skin. Old skin was black, new skin Navy gray, and the patches of color alternated like those in camouflage clothing.

Rocking in the wake of the whale was not an unpleasant sensation. Bill liked it. Some of the turbulence came, he judged, from the whale's bulk as it passed, but most of it rolled back from the flukes.

. . .

Tilting its flukes sharply for a banking turn, the whale came back. The barnacled head, the black graffitoed wall, passed him once again.

"If you reached out to touch them, they'd pull the pectoral fin in, just the way they avoided you with the flukes. Not quick, but slowly. They're frightened, but they don't want you touching them. The eye follows you. You can't read the mood. They're not expressive eyes. You can only see one at a time, for one thing. They look right through you. Geez, it's just incredible. That one eye. That grapefruit eye."

The eye rotated up toward Bill and focused as best it could. A small, blurred Bill Curtsinger, his fair skin and blond hair dazzling, fell on the retinal screen within the armored orbit. The whale saw a bright mote against a green heaven.

Right-whale eye, Patagonia

Wake of the Whale

text by Kenneth Brower

photographs by William R. Curtsinger

Friends of the Earth · New York, London, Paris

ISBN : 0-525-22950-7

Foreword

FREEDOM, for one of Romaine Gary's characters in *The Roots of Heaven*, is a place so open and wide and untrammeled that elephants can roam untroubled there from horizon to horizon and beyond. Elephants once knew that freedom. So did buffalo, wolf, and caribou, all in our own time.

The condor once had that kind of freedom in the California sky. From the Coast Ranges south of Monterey, eastward along the Tehachapis, and north to the old sequoias of the Sierra Nevada, an array of thermals and knowledge of how to use them kept the huge birds aloft, by the hundreds, even in the lifetime of some of us, and let them patrol their vast mountain arc.

And the great whales knew the one great ocean, with its coves of many names, for the countless eons when there was true freedom of the seas.

Then the different flood came, as humanity reached its first billion and passed it—the flood that seemed to need no stemming. That flood, as it surged ever higher, extinguished old freedoms. What replaced them was not a new freedom, but license, an arrogant assumption that no title to a place was valid unless written in a newly invented language by one of the most recent arrivals on the planet.

For this new flood there was no new Ark. It is already too late for a horde of splendid creatures—and for how many lesser ones we never knew?—to find sanctuary. The miraculous flow of information in their wild genes, their unique chemistries, and their love of life will not be known again. We banished them forever with a wanton wave of the hand.

Thoreau was troubled by this when he recorded in his journal, on March 23, 1856, that "the nobler animals have been exterminated here,—the cougar, panther, lynx, wolverine, wolf, bear, moose, deer, the beaver, the turkey," leaving him a tamed and emasculated country, a maimed and imperfect nature like "a tribe of Indians that had lost all its warriors." He concluded with one of his finest paragraphs:

"I seek acquaintance with Nature,—to know her moods and manners. Primitive Nature is the most interesting to me. I take infinite pains to know all the phenomena of the spring, for instance, thinking that I have here the entire poem, and then, to my chagrin, I hear that it is but an imperfect copy that I possess and have read, that my ancestors have torn out many of the first leaves and grandest passages, and mutilated it in many places. I should not like to think that some demigod had come before me and picked out some of the best of the stars. I wish to know an entire heaven and an entire earth."

Whatever Thoreau's ancestors may have mutilated, his contemporaries were extirpating whales, the sea's grandest passages, as *Moby Dick* revealed in 1851. It was rapidly becoming less than an entire sea by 1961, when a sixteen-year-old's composition looked anew at Melville and saw how fast other leaves were being torn out:

"The crew of the *Pequod* and its Captain Ahab have much the same attitude toward the white whale Moby Dick as mankind has had toward the forces of nature—the strange mixture of admiration, awe, and hate . . .

"The whole *Pequod*'s company, even Ahab, stares in wonder and admiration as Moby Dick first breaches, but, seconds later, the boats are lowered for the chase, with the intent to kill the whale or perish. All speculation about the unknown depths at which the monster feeds and about the miracle which created him are forgotten. The only thought is to bury harpoons into sides which took untold millions of years to evolve. . . .

"The compulsion to dominate nature has no practical purpose. It is no instinct necessary to man's survival, no trait imparted to him by the process of evolution. No species must conquer its environment to live successfully within its limits. Until recently it has not been hinted that this quirk of the human mind might perhaps be suicical. . . .

"So it could well be with man, unless he quickly comes to realize that he is a product and a part of his environment. If he forgets this, and continues his subjugation of nature, breaking contact with an evolutionary cycle observable now only in wilderness, he will find himself alone. . . . Whether by misjudging the power of his bombs or exhausting his natural resources in feeding his exploding population, man will destroy himself as inevitably as Ahab did.

"And his environment will have the last word. Just as the troubled sea settled above the spot where the *Pequod* sank, so life in its simplest forms would begin anew."

The young writer of 1961 is the author of *Wake of the Whale*, the current enquiry into how Bill Curtsinger, in the course of ten year's photography under the sea's surface, has almost become a marine mammal himself. From that experience, Bill amassed an unequaled collection of photographs. He asked if we wanted to do a book with him and we did. The book would immerse the readers, surround them, with the world he saw and photographed, or which escaped his lens but Kenneth Brower remembered. It would tell of the great difficulty of getting where you must be to photograph a whale—an animal not likely to come back and pose for you again if you miss the picture the first time, but willing to lift a fluke to avoid harming you in passing by. A remarkable exhibit of creatures of the sea has been indeed hunted and captured, but not towed away except on Bill Curtsinger's film. And Kenneth Brower has remarkably portrayed the unassuming man who slipped below the junction of sea and sky, and kept swimming there until his sense could tell ours of wonders we had not dreamed of.

It will take a good many Noahs, beyond those now at work in many organizations and many lands, to save whales from the latter-day flood, to succeed where the limited institutions described in Dr. Sidney Holt's introduction have faltered. *Wake of the Whale*, we should like to hope, will enhance the opportunity for the rest of us to keep intact what remains in the sea, to prevent a wake *for* the whale, for other cetaceans, and for their distant relatives, including ourselves.

DAVID R. BROWER, *Founder*
Friends of the Earth

Berkeley, California
April 9, 1979

Introduction

OF ALL MARINE animals, whales and dolphins have been the most conspicuous in literature and remain the most exciting to watch. They are superbly adapted to their world and are living indicators of its health. If their wellbeing is assured, then ocean life is likely to be secure. When the cetaceans are in danger, the ocean is too, and so is all life, including our own.

It is hard to imagine any natural danger to the great whales throughout the era preceding history except time, the enemy of all living things that follow the sexual route to diversity and continuity of line. But cetaceans have contended with time successfully.

In the early history of human societies, some cetaceans were quasi-religious symbols. The orca was a special animal to Amerindians of the Northwest Coast. The Chukchi people of northeastern Siberia believed that a great bowhead whale was the common ancestor of the Eskimo, other polar seafarers, and themselves. To the Tongans, the arrival of the humpback whales signaled the yam-planting season. The beautiful Indonesian dancer and sorceress, Tia, was reincarnated as lumba-lumba, the spinning dolphin. In the South Pacific the cult of whales is pervasive, as might be expected in a region of seafaring peoples. Drawings and carvings of whales abound on Easter Island, presumably informed by strandings and live encounters. To the Maori the whale was known as Te-ika-pipiha-nui, the great spouting fish of the God of the sea.

For the ancient peoples of the Mediterranean, dolphins were symbols of the liberation of the soul from the body; they accompanied the spirit into the hereafter. The Minoans depicted the Euoprosyne dolphin in their frescoes. On the frescoes of Thera it was joined by the common dolphin.

The dolphin cult had reached the mainland of Greece from Crete, perhaps when Apollo Delphinus, with his son Acadius, was carried by a dolphin to the navel of the earth, where he built the temple of Delphi. Later, Phalonthos or Taras, a son of Poseidon and founder of Tarentum, was rescued from the sea on a dolphin's back. The pirates who tried to hijack Dinonysus, terrified by his black magic, jumped into the Aegean and were instantly transformed into dolphins. A dolphin leaping within a crescent symbolised the harbour of the city of Messina. Another, twined on a trident, was important to Constantinople. All are immortalized on silver coins. The "King of fishes and Lord of the sea" was portrayed as the great friend of mankind, and it could be said that "to hunt the dolphin is displeasing to the Gods."

Throughout all but the last moments of their evolution, whales never met with any natural phenomenon like man. When they met him, according to Melville and others, they resisted him. The day after Captain Scammon took two gray whales on the first day in his lagoon, whales that could not avoid his boats promptly turned and attacked them, and were thereupon called devil fish. Young whales still approach boats until warned by their mothers that it is unwise to address strangers. Fear of man seems to have been learned by cetaceans, not acquired by instinct.

Our own times can bring a change. The blue whale has now become the symbol of a world-wide movement to reverse the processes of environmental destruction. The gray whale's recovery is a fine example of how past wrongs can be righted by decisive protective action. But the bare survival of the right whale, the humpback, and the blue, even under protection, serves as a grim warning that the damage caused by the ignorant or wanton may not be reversible. And the mediaeval image of the whale, grotesque and fearsome, drawn in still-death as it appears on the flensing deck or strand, unfortunately lingers on in books, on posters, on postage stamps, and in minds.

Until the United Nations Conference on the Human Environment, held in Stockholm in 1972, cetaceans were numbers to me, big numbers, living marine resources to be assessed and exploited. 'Rational exploitation' and 'sustainable yield' were key phrases invented and used by biologist-philosophers to convince the world that trees, fish, and other wildlife should be so managed as to offer material benefits to humanity. Scientists sought, by measuring, scraping, probing, and by constructing mathematical models of living populations, to learn how they multiplied, grew, and died in order to advise how the maximum benefits might be attained.

There are far fewer forests in the world now, however; more of the fishes are overfished, and wildlife species steadily diminish—owing primarily to overconfidence in our ability to predict the behavior of complex living systems and to weakness of the institutions through which people of many nations seek to achieve common goals. As

Michael Graham, a pioneer in conservation, said to the first United Nations conference on whaling in 1947, "The world does not stand still while specialists put their minds in order." The whaling industry likewise has not stood still. After eliminating the big whales, it moved on to the sei whale, to the much smaller minke, and began to look eagerly at the sei's subtropical cousin, the Bryde's whale.

The whale tribe as a whole is now far worse off than it was in 1959 when, with a few others, I was asked to help the International Whaling Commission (IWC) out of a crisis. We blew the whistle in behalf of the blue whales and humpbacks. Six years later, the IWC declared those species protected. Some whaling countries, however, were not bound by IWC rules, and some other countries lent their flags to still other whaling vessels. The whales were poorly protected, but scientists continued unwittingly to nurture optimism. Others, however, seeing the plight of whales as part of widespread but correctable degradation of the biosphere, called for a moratorium on all commercial whaling.

The IWC responded with a New Management Policy. If a population of baleen whales, the edible kind, could be shown to have been reduced by whaling to less than fifty-four per cent of the number the scientists thought had been there originally, the population would be protected. Under the new policy the scientists had to count all the whales every year. The live-body count was, more often than not, fewer in successive years; but this was conveniently construed to be due to double-counting the previous year. The mirage of 'maximum sustainable yield' for each separate stock began to dissipate as it was seen that sei whales grew faster and matured sooner when fin whales were fewer; that minke whales increased as blue whales decreased; that all were linked in the Southern Ocean with the populations of the seals, penguins, krill-eating fish, and perhaps the squid.

In December 1978 the IWC Scientific Committee, having been convened four times in eighteen months to assess and reassess the sperm whales of the North Pacific, declared that they could neither count them nor determine if there was a surplus of males but that it was better not to catch any more females. The whalers complained that they could not distinguish a live sperm female from a male. If allowed to kill both they could thereupon tell the difference. The state of the art of assessing the state of the whale could thus be seen to consist of some hard data, some soft theory, a little knowledge, and a heap of speculation.

Most predictions of yield depend on estimates of how many whales there were before whaling began and how rapidly their numbers have declined. Those estimates in turn depend on the ratio of the numbers caught to the effort expended in catching them—how many catcher boats, how many days the boats worked, how big and powerful they were, and how much their size and efficiency had increased over the period of whaling. That sounds reasonable, but there are no data from the beginning of large-scale whaling in the 19th century or data from earlier times. It is not clear how much the advances in technology change the equation—as for example when technology beats whales at their own game by echo-locating them and exploiting the limits of their submergence time, fleeing speed, and dodging skill. As the numbers of whales decline, each catcher boat, being able to chase, kill, and tow fewer whales from day to day and year to year, can spend more daylight hours searching for whales. Efficiency is increased but not the number of whales. Other variables have not been accommodated. How much more efficient do whalers become as they learn more about where the whales usually are? Do whales inhabit a smaller area as their number declines, increasing their density deceptively? A theoretical count has severe limits. We do not know how many whales there are. We pretend to know.

We ought also to know their ages. The middle ear of the baleen whales can tell us; it does not collapse under pressure and conducts sound well under water because it is plugged with wax, which is layered as the whales migrate annually between warm waters and cool. We can count the layers. The sperm whales lay down rings in their teeth. These too we can count. But we cannot count layers or rings in the living whale. Unfortunately, thousands of ear plugs and teeth lie on laboratory shelves waiting to be read. So do ovaries, barrels of them, wait to tell us whether a female was mature and how many calves she had carried. How many of those calves were born alive, survived the period of lactation, and received enough parental care to mature and continue the cycle of life? We do not know and have as yet no means of knowing. Some scientists think there is need for more specimens from which to determine ages and pregnancy rates. It seems easier to take more samples for science than to study the ones already taken. Samples are worth money; under the rules they must be butchered and the parts fully utilized. And as one Commissioner puts it: "The scientists tell us that there are tens of thousands of whales in the sea but that we can only safely take a few hundred. Must the rest be left to rot?"

We have an inkling of what is going on in the natural systems of which baleen whales are part. When there are fewer whales, and hence more food per whale until someone else eats it, the survivors grow faster and become sexually mature younger, and when they are mature the females become pregnant more often. We do not know if there are compensating changes in the rate at which they die from natural causes.

As for sperm whales, we have less than an inkling. We make do with shrewd guesses. We think they may be shortening their reproductive cycle. We do not think they mature younger, although we cannot be sure. Reducing their number may not mean there are more squid for them to eat; the squid may be eating each other. We have just noticed that males are bigger, live shorter lives, and become sexually mature later than females. The surplus of males might not be so great as we once naively hoped. The practice and regulation of sperm whaling nevertheless assumes that there are surplus males and that two thirds of them are too old, too young, not aggressive enough, or not smart enough to service females and should serve man instead. Only the dominant males and a few hopeful replacements should be left to carry on nature's good work. Add a few females for good measure.

In a nutshell, scientists try harder, but their efforts are quite inadequate. Informed by them, the new IWC policy provides so little safeguard against serious error that some people suggest that there should be whale sanctuaries. For years the IWC did maintain one in the Southeast Pacific section of the Southern Ocean. A trouble with sanctuaries, however, is that after a time more whales live inside than outside. The IWC abolished its sanctuary in 1955, and not too soon from the point of view of relentless whalers, considering how few big baleen whales remained elsewhere by then.

The International Union for the Conservation of Nature and Natural Resources has, with the World Wildlife Fund, renewed the call for sanctuaries. It wants them in many parts of the world. They would include small areas critical to the survival of particular species of whales, as is the lagoon system of Baja California, for the breeding of the gray whale, and big areas to include the full migratory range of some of the large species, such as the Southeastern Indian Ocean, from just south of the Equator to the polar ice. Sanctuaries would also protect whales from being taken alive or harassed, and would protect food supplies and habitat quality.

The heart of the matter, however, is that whaling is by no means the only threat to whales. Pollution is another. Oil spills do not help. Baltic seals abort their pups from excess of PCBs; perhaps dolphins do too. Whales entering the Mediterranean are likely to be badly burned by chemical wastes. Dumped radioactivity, explosives, and chemical weapons must surely affect the deep-diving species, such as the bottlenose and sperm whales. Fishing is an immediate and perhaps greater threat. Seals, dugongs, dolphins, and whales get entangled in fishing nets and drown. Joanna Gordon Clark has predicted, in considering the proposed krill fishery in the Antarctic, that if the fishery really gets going, baleen whales may be classed as pests. All over the world, fishermen and even navies are out gunning for marine mammals: for dolphins off Greece and Japan, for sea lions frolicking in ring-nets off Southern Africa, for orcas in the North Atlantic. Fishing could also, in the long run, reduce food supply so much as to prevent whales from recovering from previous depletion. Oceanaria are a danger. To catch one orca for exhibition may mean that several are killed or detrimentally harassed. Dr. Paul Spong has said that a live orca may now be worth nearly a quarter of a million dollars (perhaps twenty times as much as a dead Bryde's whale)—a substantial incentive to evade the US Marine Mammal Act and similar troublesome laws.

The attitude we should now take toward marine mammals was explored in 1978 by Sir Sydney Frost and his assistants. The Government of Australia asked him to conduct an independent inquiry into whales and whaling, and he did so with exemplary thoroughness. Whether or not his conclusion that Australia should seek a worldwide ban of whaling is accepted, his report in a model of humane weighing of a multitude of facts, theories, and opinions. The report also considers the intelligence and aesthetic value of cetaceans. A similar world-wide inquiry is needed on behalf of all marine mammals. Meanwhile the list of threats to them lengthens. No single threat need be fatal, but together the threats may well be. The dangers stem from the triumph of what Ray Dasmann calls the Biosphere People, who exploit everyone's ecosystem, over the Ecosystem People, who live within the limits of their own.

One good thing about keeping orcas, belugas, and dolphins in tanks for our amusement is that it helps us see how fast they can learn when they choose to. Helpful too have been those few adventurous souls who in recent years have jumped into the sea with them, and with humpbacks too, to see what people can learn, when they choose to, about what cetaceans have known so long. This knowing leads to a search that may provide what Donald Griffin calls "a window on the minds of animals," and may tell us something about how they feel, sense, and think. It may contribute remarkably to reintegrating ourselves with the rest of the natural world from which we were becoming alien, and lead to one of the most exciting adventures on which man has ever embarked.

SIDNEY HOLT

Nairobi, February 1979

Killer whale in kelp, Puget Sound

1. Silkie

THE OCEAN has an old allure, a song to call her exiles back. The song is coeval with life on land. It preceded ears to hear, and cortices to understand. The early reptiles, obeying simple orders from the neuron clumps they used for brains, had scarcely begun their march inland when a few heard the silent notes, broke ranks, and dully faced about. They watched their footsteps lead them back through the tide wrack, across the sand, and to the water's edge. They waded in. Feet became fins again.

The returning reptiles swam off in all directions, diversifying, filling oceanic niches. By one hundred and eighty million years ago, when dinosaurs had grown gigantic and were lumbering the land, icthyosaurs had grown gigantic and were cruising the deep. Icthyosaurs were a first attempt at dolphins and whales. They were nearly halfway there. In shape they were much like dolphins, but they lacked the dolphin's powers of mind, the dolphin's social graces. The icthyosaur, all savage teeth and tiny cranium, was a dolphin's nightmare of itself dreamed ages in advance.

Sixty million years ago, the mammals in their turn began returning. The class Mammalia had just asserted its dominance of the land's faunas, when the sea called back certain family lines. We don't know what these first volunteers looked like. The fossil record has not revealed a trace, a common fate for missing links and a kindness perhaps. The volunteers were no doubt sorry looking, like most transitional creatures. They were neither here nor there. They were fish impersonators, all dressed up in webbed feet and wet fur, the despair of their mothers, the laughingstock of the whole shore.

Yet by fifty million years ago, in the Eocene's "dawn of the recent," a time when, on land, the dawn horse, eohippus, was still the size of a terrier, sea mammals already amounted to something. The first whales, the archaeocetes, were snaking through the seas. They were creatures as outlandish as any in prehistory, but they were big. One group of archaeocetes, the zeuglodonts, included specimens almost as long as the longest of modern whales. One of the first fossils would be uncovered in Alabama. "The awe-stricken credulous slaves in the vicinity took it for the bones of one of the fallen angels," Herman Melville would write. "The Alabama doctors declared it a huge reptile, and bestowed upon it the name Basilosaurus. But some specimen bones of it being taken across the sea to Owen, the English anatomist, it turned out this alleged reptile was a whale, though of a departed species. So Owen re-christened the monster Zeuglodon, and in his paper read before the London Geological Society, pronounced it, in substance, one of the most extraordinary creatures which the mutations of the globe have blotted out of existence."

The zeuglodont was a glorification of the vertebra, a nearly endless celebration. The animal was a long and massive spinal column, with a set of jaws appended in afterthought. The hind limbs were shriveled and functionless. The zeuglodont's locomotion was probably serpentine. It resembled a sea serpent more than a modern whale. If the cold waters of Loch Ness truly hold some vestige of an older era in the sea, maybe it is an archaic whale, and not the plesiosaur that some hope to find.

The archaeocetes spread to the Pacific, Atlantic, and Antarctic; they spread, rather, to the ancestors of those oceans. The archaeocetes may have been ancestral to modern whales; more likely, though, is that archaeocetes and cetaceans sprang collaterally from a common stock.

Seas were warmer in the old days, but cruel all the same, and many lineages of sea mammals came to dead ends. A few small, torpedo-shaped zeuglodonts survived until near the end of the Oligocene, twenty-five million years ago, then died out. Desmostylus, a sort of sea-hippopotamus, foraged widely along Pacific shorelines, crushing shellfish with massive molars. It survived in large numbers until ten million years ago, then it too passed. For a while an oceangoing raccoon-dog paddled about, a brave experiment, but it sank without heirs.

Other lineages prospered. The squalodonts, a family of primitive dolphins, were fruitful and multiplied. By fifteen million years ago, when horses had reached the size of sheep, and mastodonts tramped the continents, the squalodonts had evolved skulls of a configuration close to that of modern dolphins. The ancestors of man still chattered in the trees. Newton's laws and Darwin's deductions were grunts and leafy belches. The squalodonts boasted the best of what this planet had to offer in the way of brains.

Modern marine mammals trace their descent—or *could* trace it, if they were the least interested in genealogy— back to six separate returns to the sea. The baleen whales, of which there are ten species, among them the blue, fin, right, humpback, and minke whales, are descended from a primitive hoofed mammal that was recalled to the sea sixty million years ago. The toothed whales, all sixty-four species, among them the sperm whale, various beaked whales, and the dolphins, are descended from another hoofed animal that wandered down to the ocean at about the same time—sixty million years before the present. The four species of sirenians—the manatees and dugongs —are descended from a third ungulate, which hoofed back fifty-five million years ago. The seventeen species of crawling seals, among them the harbor seal, ribbon seal, bearded seal, elephant seal, and harp seal, are descended from an otterlike carnivore that slipped into some embayment thirty million years ago. The fifteen species of walking seals—the sea lions, fur seals, and walruses—descend from a bearlike carnivore that splashed in about the same time. The sea otter, a single species, is descended from a land otter that came back five million years ago.

For warm-blooded animals, the great obstacle to the return, the ongoing problem of life in the sea, has been the cold. Thermal conductivity of water is more than twenty times that of air. Sea currents drain body heat much faster than land breezes, even in the tropics. Whales combat the cold with insulation, a blubber layer which in larger species reaches two feet in thickness. Seals employ both blubber and a coat of hair. The sea otter relies on a pelt so thick that water never penetrates to the skin. There have been adjustments, too, in circulatory systems. The veins in the flukes, fins, and flippers are arranged close to the arteries, to route warm blood back into the interior before it loses much heat to the sea. In addition, the smaller marine mammals—seals, sea otter, and porpoises—have a high metabolism. They defeat the chill by living fast.

All sea mammals are sizable, for bulk conserves heat. For mammals, the lower weight limit for individual survival in the open sea seems to be about ten pounds. In their first winter, fur seal pups sometimes get that lean. Some pups succeed in burning enough fish to keep traveling that lightly, but many don't. The failures wash up as corpses on December beaches. The smallest *adult* sea mammal is the female sea otter, which weighs seventy-five pounds. Below that weight, a mother otter would have trouble stoking aboard enough sea urchins and abalone to keep warm and raise a family at the same time.

Evolution will bring us no sea cats, then, nor sea mice. No sea rabbit will bound over the waves or snuffle along the bottom. Marine squirrels won't lay up stashes of cowries inside old wrecks or coral heads.

There won't be sea shrews. On land, a shrew must consume the equivalent of one and a half times its body weight each day. To keep home fires cheery, this tiniest of

Sea lions, Patagonia

mammals must run around ceaselessly, perpetually irritable and overamped. In the sea, shrews would be insufferable.

Sea bears are possible, though. Indeed, in the polar bear, they may be in the process of becoming. There is nothing to prevent a sea kangaroo, unless it's some natural force of propriety.

There is no law against a sea man.

As a boy Bill Curtsinger used to make scuba gear out of galvanized pipe and lengths of hose, then jump out of trees, pretending he was jumping into the ocean. It was odd behavior, for New Jersey. "I was always comfortable in the water," he remembers. "I always had that water thing, somewhere in my mind."

In high school, he found himself estranged from the society of his fellows. He did not fit in.

When he began to date, girls told him a strange thing. "All the women I've ever been involved with tell me how soft I am," he says, looking down regretfully at his waist. "I've always had a lot of baby fat." He is fit enough, but a superficial softness lingers stubbornly, immune to jogging and calisthenics. It's as if it were nature's intent.

When he reached manhood, science confirmed female observation. Curtsinger was one of a group of divers being studied in the Arctic by dive physiologists. Daily he and his colleagues swallowed pills containing thermometers and tiny radios, which were to monitor their core temperatures while they swam under the ice. Each morning, on the way to the latrine, they were given rubber gloves and instructed to pick through yesterday's meal for the pill, which was then washed off and recycled. The gastric radios did not work. The cold water seemed to affect transmission. The scientists also used calipers, which they applied to the backs of the men to measure subcutaneous fat. Coming to Billy Curtsinger, science raised an eyebrow and whistled. Billy was skinniest, yet he had more subcutaneous fat than anyone.

Bill had noticed himself that he was able to work the icy waters longer than the others.

He got married. His wife, Kate, detected his extra insulation. She called it his "love handles" and teased him about it. She was an admirer, though, of her husband's grace underwater. "Once he makes a surface dive to go down, he's just a different person," she says today. "He's just . . . well, there's not one extra motion. He doesn't flutter around. Everything is slow, not like he's stalking something, exactly, but so as not to disturb anything. It's as if he says, 'I'm underwater now; everything else in the world ceases to be important.'"

Kate is Irish-American. In Gaelic myth—in the folk tradition of her old country—there were sea men, silkies, who came ashore occasionally in human form. Is Kate prey to some of the ambivalence that the mortal mistress of a silkie must have felt toward her mate? Or is this just Kate's colleen face and an overexercise of my imagination? Colleen and overexercise, probably.

If Bill Curtsinger is a transitional creature, a primate trying to become a seal, then he is caught in an early stage of transit. His posture is sometimes slouchy, and his eyes turn down at the outside corners, but he cannot properly be called sorry looking, like the majority of those ambiguous animals fossilized on their way to someplace else. His eyes, blue and humorous, meet yours directly. His step on land is forthright. Curtsinger is a blond middleweight with large hands and a close-trimmed, reddish-blond beard. His eyebrows are so fair as to hardly be there. His skin is the thin, Nordic sort intended for use in high temperate latitudes, and he has abused the warranty, immersing his epidermis under the sea ice of both poles, exposing it in small boats to the equatorial sun. His forehead and eyes are lined from squinting into scintillations. In a decade or so, his face will be a log of all the weather it's seen, a map of all the places. For now, at thirty-two, it is just good-natured.

Curtsinger is, in his own estimation, "a visual person," not a great thinker or propounder. He considers himself inarticulate. In this he is unnecessarily hard on himself. In conversation he does have one odd habit—he repeats himself when speaking with emotion. "He came ashore to die," he will say, in describing a sea lion bull he met once on a beach in Patagonia. "He came ashore to die. Everything about him said old. He was huge, with scars from old fights. His teeth were worn. He came ashore to die. He just came ashore to die."

Curtsinger's style is natural and unstudied. He's the kind of man a sea lion or a dolphin would like—or so I like to think. I asked him once how he steadied his camera underwater. His answer, it seems to me, could have been a dolphin's explanation of its skills translated faithfully into English. "I don't know," he said. "I dunno. It's just something you do. You just sort of, you know . . . you just sort of flow smoothly along. I dunno. I dunno. You sort of steady yourself. In a sense, it's easier to steady it in the water, and in another sense it's not. It's easier in that there's more resistance to the motion of the camera, but then there's nothing to brace against. You almost swim around the camera. That's the best I can do."

For most of his career he has been a photographer of marine mammals. He doesn't know why. He did not plan things that way; he just slipped into it. Sometimes he photographs other animals—pelicans, herring, beaver—but he always seems to come back to those creatures of warm blood who preceded him home to the sea.

Bill slouches on his sofa in Maine. I sit more erect, my notebook open and resting on my knee. He has arranged it so I face inland and he faces the Atlantic, which today is overcast and windy—"feather-white," as they say in Maine. A long horizon of waves marches across the picture window behind my head. While we talk, Bill drums intermittently with a pencil on the wall behind him. He isn't interested in my questions, and in his answers he loses the thread.

For a month he has been home in Maine—an unusually long domestic interlude. He is awaiting the call for his next assignment. A scientist of his acquaintance is now searching the continental shelf for herring spawn, which Bill is to photograph when the discovery is made. Autumn is half over and the phone has not rung. For the past week, he has been fidgety, and this morning is the worst. He seems forever on the verge of shaking his head ruefully. He seems vaguely discouraged with himself.

"Whenever I find myself growing grim about the mouth," says Ishmael, on the opening page of the greatest whale story of all, "whenever it is a damp, drizzly November in my soul; whenever I find myself involuntarily pausing before coffin warehouses, and bringing up the rear of every funeral I meet; and especially whenever my hypos get such an upper hand of me, that it requires a strong moral principle to prevent me from deliberately stepping into the street, and methodically knocking people's hats off— then, I account it high time to get to sea as soon as I can."

Bill's pencil drums on the wall, and his eyes wander away.

"What's the matter, Bill?" I ask.

"Huh? Nothing." He smiles sheepishly and glances at me.

I don't let him off the hook. I fix him with a curious stare.

"Nothing," he repeats. "I don't know. Nothing." He looks past me to the window. Outside, beyond the glass, the gray ocean sings him her primeval song.

2. Argentina

SOMETIMES in the mornings, Kate, pausing to rest as she climbed the cliff to her hut, would turn and scan the broad blue expanse of gulf until she saw the gray dot of the Zodiac. If the boat was chasing after dolphins, all the participants—Billy, Bora, and the dolphins—looked to her like small boys playing tag. The men were always "it." The dolphins were always winning. The dolphins had a knack for surfacing ninety degrees from where the men expected them. Kate would watch for a while, then resume her climb.

The pale cliff, composed of sand and fossil shells, was an old sea floor elevated several hundred feet above the gulf. Its face was sheer. On top was a desert plateau. Kate's hut, built of composition board and painted shamrock green, stood on the very clifftop, a flimsy eminence, its walls buckling from the weather. Her front window looked out at Golfo San José. A side window looked along the cliffs and peeked at a blue corner of gulf. The door was in back and it opened on desert.

Kate perched there at the interface, pressed between two immensities. Out back, the world was an outback, a tableland of gnarled, chest-high trees. Darwin's rheas—three-toed American ostriches—hunted the dunes, and raptors, "hawky, kestrel-type things, birds you never saw on the beach," hunted the air. The view out back was of heartland in some improbable xeric continent.

The view out front was vertical and maritime. The birds wheeled, seabirds, and the horizon was blue and distant.

At first Kate had not been happy in Argentina. "I'm used to things being green and lush," she says. "When we came around the bend to the place we were going to stay, my heart just sank. All that brush and dryness." Kate let the flies get to her, before learning the old trick with flies, and she had suffered in having no place to work, no territory of her own. The cliff hut was perfect for that, but when they arrived it had been padlocked, and Bill and Bora had been unable to break in. Finally they found the key, and she had converted the hut to a studio. The trick with flies was to ignore them.

A wooden bed, just wide enough for the sleeping bag of a former gulf-watching tenant, had been built into one wall. This became Kate's desk. She spread Maine shells around, mementos of another hemisphere, and she hung up a couple of her old paintings. "I like to bring a few things for continuity," she explains. "Boom, suddenly you're in Argentina. It's good to have things from home."

The wind blows ceaselessly in Patagonia, and her metal roof rattled with the gusts. Aeolian erosion rubbed the cliff away and sent it in gritty groundstorms along the clifftop, sandblasting her walls. The sand found the cracks and trickled in. On leaving each afternoon, she spread a beach towel over the bed, covering her pens and sketchbooks against the perpetual motion of the grains.

The sky always held plenty of light for Kate's descent from her studio. January is the middle of Patagonian summer, and the days would last until ten in the evening. Sunsets were endless and beautiful. Coming down, Kate would hear the Zodiac before she saw it. She could tell how well the men had done with dolphins by how long they had stayed out. A long day on the water, twelve hours or so, was usually a good day.

One evening Kate had nearly reached the beach, when something made her turn. She looked up. Above her a herd of guanacos was traversing the cliff. She counted them—twenty-five. They moved effortlessly across the steep face, graceful, llamalike animals—American camels with reddish brown coats. Kate hurried down to the beach, where on level ground she could keep pace, and she followed as long as she could. She heard a guanaco whinny—a sound very like a horse's. Then they were gone.

This coast had been a good spot for observing dolphins for as long as dolphins had existed. The cliffs from which Kate and her companions watched for living animals were repositories for the bones of extinct predecessors. The three humans didn't know it—they weren't here for paleontology—but the marine formation here, along the shore of Chubut Province, held the Miocene's oldest known fossils of pelagic mammals. *Prosqualodon australis*, the shark-toothed porpoise, lay deep under their feet. So did *Phoberdon arctirostrus*, a porpoise whose specific name means "bear beak." The jaws were longer in the extinct animals, and the dentition was terrific, but the skulls were recognizably those of dolphins. In the blue gulf, beneath the steep desert tombs of their ancestors, the descendents leapt and somersaulted as if life went on forever.

In Patagonia, Bill Curtsinger wore a Merric Aviation baseball cap as protection against the sun.

Bora Merdsoy needed no cap. Bora is shorter than Bill, stockier, a few months older, and considerably darker. He is a Turk who lives now in Canada. After a few weeks in Patagonia, Bill and Kate called him Black Bora. There is no one with whom Curtsinger would rather work in the field. Bora is endlessly funny, or almost so. He puns constantly in English, his second language, and he is a fine comic actor. He is given to brief periods of moodiness, but even these are interesting, in the monotony that sometimes settles over a camp. Bora was once a diver in the Canadian Navy. He is now, when not working with Bill, a biologist. Marshall Alexander, a lobsterman Bill knows in Maine, describes Bora as "half bull, half seal," and it's a good description. Bill has complete confidence in Bora underwater, routinely trusting him with his life there.

Kate, who in Argentina was twenty-six, is a sturdy, pretty woman, a native of Massachusetts, where she went to art school. She is an Irish-American of the variety called T.T.I. (Two-Toilet Irish, she explains, is one step more affluent than Lace-Curtain Irish, two steps more than Shanty Irish.) In Patagonia she was Outhouse Irish, a temporary reversion.

The fourth member of the party was Bloater, the Zodiac. The boat was named after a friend from Maine. Bloater was a good name for a tightly inflated rubber boat. The name served also, like Kate's Maine shells and paintings, as a reminder of home. It had a pleasant English ungainliness, here on Golfo San José, on Peninsula Valdés, of Chubut Province, of Argentina.

In the mornings, on rising, Bill and Bora stepped out on the porch to scan the gulf with the spotting scope. If the weather was clear, they would usually see dolphins. On days when the weather was bad, they would not. If the tide was high, launching Bloater was easy. Often they succeeded in loading the boat with diving gear and cameras and dragging it into the water within ten minutes of sighting dolphins. But if the tide was low, launching sometimes took half an hour. The beach shelved very gradually, becoming enormous when the tide went out and making for a long portage.

Early, before the beach got too hot, Kate did yoga there, then climbed her cliff. On some mornings she carried the spotting scope for fun, just to see what her husband was up to. Other mornings she carried the scope as a duty. These were the mornings when Bill and Bora saw no dolphins, got impatient waiting—the sky clear, the blue gulf beckoning—and decided to go out anyway. On the water they were closer to the action, should any occur, but they sacrificed perspective. The big picture of the gulf they entrusted to Kate, along with a walky-talky. Before pushing off, she would synchronize watches with them and agree to regular check-in times. When those times neared, Kate, high in her hut, would set down the painting in progress and look for dolphins. The gulf played optical tricks at first, but she found that the eye, having familiarized itself with a body of water, quickly learned to pick out the things that were unusual there. Seeing a white re-entry splash, or the shine from a row of fins, she would call the coordinates down to the Zodiac: "Straight out from the house," or "just south of the point." She never stayed in communication with the boat all day. Bill and Bora would get caught up in the chase, forgetting to call in, or they would pass behind the cliff, cutting off the walky-talkies. The empty static did not make Kate sad. When check-in time came and the only message from below was a crackling, she would return happily to her work.

Her work was in collage and watercolor. There were paintings of the gulf and desert. There was a series of human figures she had begun before she left Maine, a series free of Argentine influences, as nearly as she could tell. In the Patagonian desert there were no human figures for inspiration. There were watercolors of dolphins feeding. These last, in which vortices of leaping dolphins, fleeing fish, and diving birds merge to become one another, would have seemed, to anyone unfamiliar with this gulf, wildly fanciful.

In Argentina the work had begun slowly, as is usual with cetaceans.

"Out from camp around 1 P.M. after running compressor for first time," Bill's Argentine journal begins, on January 17, 1977. "Everything seemed to be OK. Kate was a little flipped out this morning about flies and her lack of territory, etc. Everything resolved by night time with the hut. No sightings at all today from the boat, but late in the morning four or five Risso's dolphins swam in front of camp, passing back and forth several times. Obviously Risso's, with confirmation photos. Motor working well. Equipment is go. Now we need obscurus to be not so obscure."

Obscurus was *Lagenorhynchus obscurus*, the dusky dolphin, one of the three species that frequented the gulf. The other two were the bottlenose dolphin, *Tursiops truncatus*, and Risso's dolphin or the gray grampus, *Grampus griseus*.

Risso's dolphin is a big, blunt-headed animal closely resembling the pilot whale. (The pilot whale, too, is a dolphin—the second-largest dolphin of all, after the killer whale.) Risso's dolphin, like the pilot whale, is shy. Underwater it looks pale and it always seems to be moving away from you. Risso's dolphins are distinguished by scratches on their backs and dorsal fins. "Something goes on with those animals," says Bill. "They all wind up with those scratches. They cover their whole bodies."

On January 20, Risso's dolphins passed close to the beach. The tide was up, and the Zodiac was in the water within ten minutes. Bill and Bora maneuvered for two hours to get into position for underwater photographs, but were unsuccessful. Bill did see three Risso's dolphins swim by at the edge of visibility. One circled back and bobbed its head at him several times, forcing a stream of bubbles from its blowhole. Bill has noted this head-bobbing in many of the marine mammals he has photographed, and he has seen bubble-blowing in almost all of them. Both are warnings, he believes.

On January 22, they caught up with Risso's dolphins again. This time the animals seemed less troubled by the boat, and less shy of Bill when he eased into the water. One came very close, and again bubbles came from the blowhole. Bill wished the water were clearer. The dolphins began moving off, this time slowly enough that he could swim along, though too far behind for photographs. Giving up finally on underwater pictures, he took surface shots—scarred gray backs with the golden, crumbling cliff behind.

When the dolphins began to act nervous, he quit. Bill Curtsinger is not pushy with his subjects. He once began a photo essay for *National Geographic* on the outrigger-canoe culture of Micronesia, but found it nearly impossible to shove his camera into the honest faces of native islanders. He was the wrong man for the job and he got no good pictures. He is respectful, too, in his approach to sea mammals, and there, sometimes, it pays off. With Risso's dolphin it did not. His diplomacy notwithstanding, he was to get no underwater photographs of *Grampus griseus*.

He and Bora returned to shore. They resumed their dolphin watch. No dolphins appeared, and, getting bored, Bill and Bora launched Bloater again. They were heading for Los Conos, a steep-sided peninsula immediately northeast of camp, when they came upon dusky dolphins feeding. The dolphins were moving a school of fish along, and an excited storm of birds—gulls and terns—was following. Of the birds, the terns were the more efficient and in control, diving just ahead of the dolphins and coming up often with fish. They wheeled, screamed, and dove again. Bloater's outboard whined to keep up.

Ahead, a dense, circular flock of gulls sat on the water. Watching, Bill saw them all lift off in unison and plunge their beaks in, many grabbing fish, just as a dolphin surfaced nearby. He observed this again, then again and again; the birds waiting, crowded and expectant, then rising like a single animal and stabbing for fish, just as the glistening fin of a dolphin broke the surface. Could the dolphins be herding fish for the birds? And if so, why? He hadn't the remotest idea.

He spit into his mask and rubbed the glass, defogging it, then pulled the strap back over his head. When the moment seemed right—the birds thick and excited, yet not moving so fast as before, the flock's shape not shifting so kaleidoscopically, the schooling fish beneath relatively stationary—he swung his legs over and slipped in.

Underwater he was instantly surrounded by dolphins. They seemed very excited on having him with them, and raced around like dervishes. Turning his head, he recorded only glimpses, single frames of action. Future dives would permit him to make these frames into a movie, but for now he was confused. He saw dolphins streaking. He saw a dense wall of anchovy, frantic, but still bound together by the schooling instinct, turning as a unit. Now attenuated, now a silver bolus, the school darkened or lightened as the fish unanimously altered course. He saw a dolphin passing through the school. Its sleek, pale form was broken into mosaic by the smaller, interlocking, for-the-moment-darker forms of fish. Then everything was gone, the hunt having passed on, the ocean blue and empty. It might have been a dream, except for the silver scales of fish. They made a gentle snowfall, swirling in the last turbulence of the departed host, then slowing, then beginning a downward drift.

Bill's underwater view of the dolphins had been dim and sketchy. The dolphins' view of Bill had been anything but.

The dolphins' Curtsinger was multi-dimensional and richly detailed. Their first glimpse was auditory—his splash on entering the water. Echolocating, they sent bursts of clicks toward the disturbance, lower frequencies to rough Bill out, higher frequencies to fill in his details. They produced their sounds in a manner for the most part still unknown. They can do it without exhaling, thereby saving air, and they seem to make use of the "melon," an oil-filled chamber behind the forehead. They are capable of sounds so intense that the skull behind the melon is thickened to protect the thought processes from fragmentation by the noise. They can reel off three hundred clicks a second. Here, in Golfo San José, some click sequences were spaced so that the outgoing clicks would not interfere with incoming echoes, and some sequences were spaced so that the echoes *would* interfere, allowing the dolphin to learn about Curtsinger by interpreting the interference patterns.

The dolphins received the echoes with their jawbones and their melons—odd organs of hearing, but efficient just the same, capable of detecting higher tones than the gear of any animal but the bat. With their jaws, the dolphins could detect the direction of origin of underwater sound, as Bill's ears could not. Human ears are a stereo system designed for hearing in the air. They work because the human head is a thousand times denser than air. Sound—vibrations in the air—is channeled through the air-filled canal of the outer ear to the inner ear's receiver. The slight lag in arrival time at the leeward ear, and the difference in volume, allows us to determine the direction of the source. The system is no good when flooded. The human head is only eight times denser than water, and that disparity is not enough; instead of entering the two proper inlets, underwater sound enters everywhere. The whole head vibrates in sympathy, and there is no clue as to source. In dolphins the ears have been reduced to pinholes; instead sound enters the jawbone, travels inside the bone through a canal filled with an oil considerably less dense than water, then passes through the "acoustic window," an oval of paper-thin bone at the rear of the jaw, then proceeds to the inner ear. Simultaneously, or nearly so, the same vibrations are passing through the oil reservoir in the melon and thence to the inner ear.

While each dolphin analyzed Bill, it was at the same time able to keep track of the school of fish and to chart the courses its fellow dolphins were taking. For the moment, Curtsinger was in sharper focus than these other concerns, which began to blur and fade, like blips on a sonar screen after the scanner has passed. The cloud of fish, and the denser and faster blips of fellow dolphins, glowed milkily on the screen of each dolphin's memory, waiting to be renewed when its beak swung that way again.

Humans can echolocate too, in a rudimentary way. Echolocation guides us past furniture in darkened rooms, halting us before we hit the sofa or the wall. Near objects pass as a sort of looming. We whistle in the dark. We know from the echoes of our footsteps whether we have stumbled into some great marble hall, or into a small and overstuffed apartment. But where we slide our feet forward cautiously, always anticipating a bump, dolphins tear through gleefully at twenty knots. The coffee tables we curse darkly in their black seas are sharks.

Possessing the faculty in a primitive way, we can guess at how its refinement feels in dolphins. If the dolphin's sense is anything like our own, objects are experienced as pressures. The sensation is tactile yet remote. For a dolphin, the pressures are exquisitely modeled, and here is where our intuition breaks down. Trying to imagine details in a topography of pressure takes heroic effort, for a

Diviner than the dolphin is nothing yet created; for indeed they were aforetime men and lived in cities along with mortals, but by the devising of Dionysos they exchanged the land for the sea and put on the form of fishes.

—OPPIAN

Dusky dolphin leaping, sunset, Patagonia

Dolphin societies are extraordinarily complex, and up to ten generations coexist at one time. If that were the case with man, Leonardo da Vinci, Faraday, and Einstein would still be alive.

—PROFESSOR YABALOV

Dusky dolphins and anchovies

human, and is fruitless, like trying to imagine the features on the face of God. We don't have the equipment.

The sonar screen is a diminishing metaphor, in a discussion of dolphin capabilities. On human sonar, whale-sized objects show up as bright smears. On dolphin sonar, the resolution is far better, with individual anchovies distinguishable. On human sonar, the submarine world, reconstructed, flickers two-dimensionally on the glass. With dolphin sonar, the world is reconstructed in three dimensions. The dolphin system is especially sensitive to motion. Movement toward the dolphin or away from it is marked by a Doppler effect, so that motion jumps out at the dolphin from a background of static presences, just as motion jumps out at us from a background of color.

Dolphin sensibilities have the power to penetrate matter. If an object holds reasonably still, dolphins will take a look inside. Bill's dolphins read him as an X-ray would. The sharp vibrations of their clicks entered him, rebounding differentially from organs of different densities. Curtsinger's dolphin audience may have been able to watch his bones articulate as he swam toward them. They surely saw his lungs, big air cavities a thousand times less dense than the thorax surrounding them. Perhaps this X-ray image of lungs—this Dolphin-ray image—explained their excitement over him. Perhaps they instantly recognized his kinship. Lungs are rare in the sea, possessed only by cetaceans, seals, diving birds, sea turtles and snakes, and it must be nice to see a new set. Perhaps this instant recognition of a familiar respiratory apparatus helps explain those incidents in which dolphins push struggling swimmers to shore.

Bill's dolphins reached a judgment about him in an instant, and surrounded him before he knew it. Moving close, they verified him with their eyes.

"They were *excited* when you got in the water?" I asked him, months later.

"Yes. They do get excited. They get excited. You notice the excitement in the motion of their bodies. They're excited. They have an expressionless face, like all whales and dolphins, but they swim fast around. They get *excited*. They're just excited. They're excited. You sense they're excited. They're excited."

Remembering dolphins, Bill was getting excited himself. He didn't hear his repetition. He seemed to think he was imparting a different nuance to the word with each delivery.

"They get excited. They'll swim around very rapidly. I almost think sometimes they want you to swim with them. When they see you can't, they lose interest. You can't get in the game with them.

"That's why they ride the bow of a boat—of an out-board. They're excited by that kind of movement. It's *fast.* They're excited. They're excited. They don't ride the bow to feed, or anything. They're just excited by this thing riding through the water almost as fast as they can. They're excited.

"I'm not expressing it. I'm not using the right words.

"They *relate* to that motion—that's sort of the word I'm looking for. They *relate* to that; they're familiar with that. And they definitely get excited when you get in the water. They definitely get excited. I just wonder why they get excited. I know they get excited, but *why* do they get excited?"

The Golfo San José dolphins, on seeing that Bill wasn't going to follow, turned away. Curtsinger's blip blurred and faded on their screens. The school of fish jumped again into focus and relief, a multitude of blips that slimmed instantly into the slivers of anchovies. The dolphins took off. Bill was left behind in the gentle rain of silver scales.

"Mussels completely covered the rocks there," Kate remembers. "They made the rocks black, soft, velvety-looking. The beach was really wide at low tide. When the tide was out, we sometimes hunted octopus in the rocks at the point but mostly we ate mussels. We ate an awful lot of mussels there."

Dominican gulls, wearing black-and-white habits, hunted the rocks, too. The dominicans conducted inquisitions all along the exposed tidal flats. When the tide was high, the flats shrank, so the gulls withdrew to theologize in large gatherings at their favorite spot on the beach. Oyster-catchers, which Bill decided were his favorite Argentine birds, hunted in pairs, probing the sand with their bright red bills. Grebes worked the waters off the beach, along with Magellanic penguins, black-browed albatrosses, skuas, jaegers, and two species of tern. Sometimes on the beach, a penguin would waddle into the dominican huddle, a temporary conversion. Sometimes a pair of cormorants would rest there too, wings held up to dry. The oyster-catchers' cries were shrill. The penguins' calls were high-pitched too, carrying well over the water. The cormorants, which nested at Los Conos, had a peculiar and insistent cry, *errll, errll, errll.* ("You Earl?" Bora inquired of Bill as they passed the point one day.)

Following the example of the dolphins and birds, Bill and Bora fished for anchovies off the beach. They used a fine-mesh net. One man walked close to shore, the other deeper in the surf. The outer man would turn in, and they would bring the net together, heavy with fish. They ate their anchovies breaded, and they ate them on pizza, which

Gulls and dusky dolphin, Patagonia

Bill learned to make from scratch in Patagonia. (Argentina had great pepperoni, as well as great anchovies, so pizza was inevitable.)

Outside the house was an *asado* pit surrounded by a circular windbreak of brush. In the pit they barbecued hunks of Argentine beef they bought in the interior. Their method was Stone Age. They cooked the meat until they could slice some off, then returned it to the fire to cook some more. Armadillos had burrowed beneath the windbreak and during meals they would make their appearance. The armadillos of Peninsula Valdés were tame enough to eat from the hand, though they scooted off at any quick movement. Sometimes Bill held out a rib and played tug of war. "If you held the bone too long, they'd go into stylized behavior," he says. "They'd run to the burrow and dig dirt at you. They were fantastic diggers. They could dig into sand and disappear as fast as sand crabs."

Armadillos made good eating, the Argentines said, and their burrows, right by the barbecue pit, could not have been more convenient, but Bill and his party never considered that.

On February 5, after a week of wind, the weather cleared.

Out on the sunny gulf, amidst a flurry of screaming seabirds, Bill Curtsinger slipped over the side to find himself, finally, where for weeks he had been trying to maneuver—close to the heart of the dolphin feeding frenzy.

"The whole time," he says, "we had been trying to get into the center of activity, and not succeeding. Oftentimes we'd get in the water and see nothing but scales. It had all been there a moment before, and now it was gone.

"If you take a boat into the middle, the frenzy will disperse; so you take the boat to the fringe, and get in the water, and hope you haven't disturbed it. Usually the dolphins move off. You swim back to the boat and try it again—dozens of times.

"Oftentimes the group we were with would start up suddenly, all in the same direction, and join another group feeding two miles away. Instantly, and simultaneously, and all at the exact, same, precise moment, they would take off at top speed in the same direction. There has to be some signal that organizes all that. We would be left behind."

The swirl of action meandered capriciously and fast, like a dust devil or a waterspout, and it ended soon after it began. Bill and Bora had to catch up quickly. Once the dolphins had had a few minutes with the densely herded school of anchovies, the school broke up into fragments and dispersed.

Bill tried ambushes. He would swim in scuba tanks beneath a ball of fish, looking up through his viewfinder, waiting and waiting. The sun danced above, its image spalled into the images of thousands of fish. The bubbles from his regulator wobbled up brightly, joining the school. The fish shifted lazily, the school protean and dazzling in his watery heaven. No avenging angels of dolphins appeared.

Now, as he moved at last toward the fishy tornado, Bill knew what he was seeing. In previous days he had observed enough in bits and pieces to be able to sort out the confusion.

The heart of the storm was always beneath the most excited birds. The birds were dominican gulls, cormorants, albatrosses, and the two species of tern. There were jaegers too, which chased after and mugged successful

Black-browed albatrosses

Dusky dolphins and anchovies

working birds. Occasionally the albatrosses left off their honest fishing to do some mugging of their own. Bill had identified them all before, and today in a glance he took attendance. Then for twenty minutes he swam about, trying to position himself correctly under them.

Underwater, he now recognized the shape of the herded school as a cylinder. The dolphins had sculpted it that way for their convenience, racing around in circles, occasionally breaking off to make a pass through the anchovies. The dolphins entered and exited the school like wraiths passing through a wall. In the space of a three-second pass, he estimated, a dolphin would take two fish. The duskies were so quick he could not see their mouths open; the fish just disappeared. The fish couldn't keep track of the duskies, and neither could Bill. "You can't follow a dolphin swimming around you—you just can't. It's not like in air. You're moving your head around against the resistance of the water, and besides, the face mask limits your peripheral vision. They're just like race cars going by. Zoom zoom zoom. And on a very small track."

The upper end of the cylinder was bright and frothy as the seabirds preyed upon it. Through his viewfinder he saw, amidst explosions of bubbles, a webbed foot here, a lunging beak there.

He could not swim fast enough to keep up, but occasionally his own course, more or less purposeful, and the

erratic courselessness of the cylinder collided. He entered the maelstrom. No one had been there before. Dazed fish bumped into his face mask. He found he could reach out and grab confused anchovies himself.

Something seized his ankle, and the shock traveled up his spine. His first thought was that a dolphin had bitten him, breaking the treaty between them, and his next thought was *shark*. He looked back to see beak and black brow of an albatross.

As the action seethed around him, Curtsinger tried to keep calm.

"I was worrying about the exposures, and trying to bracket the pictures. I didn't bracket enough, it turned out. A lot of those pictures are hot. Overexposed. Because of the bubbles from the birds. The bubbles were bouncing light around.

"The camera is capturing part of it, and your memory is getting the rest. Coming out, that's what you think about—a combination of the pictures you just got, or hoped you did, and what you had seen. There was this overwhelming sense of how great it was. I couldn't even talk, a couple of times with Bora. I couldn't talk to him at all. I was laughing, but I couldn't talk."

Curtsinger sprawled in the boat, wet, sunburned, ecstatic. When he found his voice, he could only say,

"I can't tell you, Bora. I just can't tell you."

3. Antipool

AT THE FOOT OF THE PIER sit tangled dunes of line, lobster traps, and bright-painted buoys, all snarled by the storm. At the end of the pier, lobster boats are unloading. The rain has stopped, finally, but the sky is gray, the day cool. Bill alights from his old Volvo and stares for a moment at the boats in Cape Porpoise harbor. He looks down at the snarled line. He nudges it with his boot. "Here they call this 'warp'," he informs me. Then he comes to himself and we walk out on the pier.

It is a Saturday in late October, and we are ten miles south of Biddeford Pool, Maine, Bill Curtsinger's adopted home. Biddeford Pool lies at the same latitude north of the equator that Golfo San José lies south of it. The two bodies of water are antipodes, or antipools. In Golfo San José, at this moment, summer is approaching; here in Maine, winter.

Bill is so seldom home in Maine that he sometimes is uncertain what to do with himself here. He has spent the morning just driving around.

The pier manager, a friend of Bill's, sees us coming and stops work. He is Hale Whitehouse, a big, hale, square-jawed man in his forties. For me Hale is an unfamiliar type. To my parched California eye his features belong in some Old World, gray-skied place. The Aran Islands, maybe. Maine's bracing climate has flushed his cheeks and tightened his skin—there is nothing soft about him —but his face is pale. In California, fishermen are browner.

The two men talk of the fishing. They talk of the weather. They talk of all the traps the storm has snarled. They speak of scuba-diving to unsnarl traps. Hale asks what Bill charges for that. "Nothing," Bill admits. He dives only occasionally, for friends, he says. Sometimes he gets lobsters in exchange. "What did *you* charge?" he asks Hale.

"I had a ten-dollar minimum. And that was several years ago."

Hale excuses himself and returns to work. Bill, watching his friend's broad back as it recedes from us, turns and confides, "He used to dive all the time. It's too bad. He has a collapsed lung. He used to spend hours in the water, all by himself."

We walk to the dock's edge and peer over. A new boat has come alongside, and below us lobstermen in raingear are lifting boxes of lobsters onto a small winch. The boxes creak up topside, where other lobstermen offload and carry them into a shed. One of the topside men stops beside us, a box of lobsters in his arms. He is Gary Ridlon, another friend of Bill's. The two got drunk together three years ago at Bill's wedding. Gary wears yellow rubber overalls, a dark sweater, and a wool watch cap. He grins at Bill impishly. "Are you on vacation?" he asks. His Maine accents are strong.

"You know me, I'm always on vacation."

It's an old joke, apparently. Bill's life is backwards; when he is home he is on vacation. The lobsterman is making fun of the photographer's career of constant travel, and Bill plays along, but jokes like this bug him a little. Gary, as if sensing this, changes tack. His eyes get a little more sober. "You've been around here this summer?" he asks.

"No. I've been away most of the summer."

The lobsters are getting heavy. Gary shifts the weight and begins moving off toward the shed, then pauses with a thought. "Do you need an assistant in the South Pacific this winter?"

"Yeah. Do you want to come?"

"Hell yes, I'll come."

"What will your wife say?"

"If I'm with you, she won't worry."

Gary disappears into the shed. Bill's eyes wander, then settle on a lobster boat anchored out. The boat has a high bow, like salmon boats on my coast. It looks to be good in rough weather. "I love the lines of that boat," he says.

"I always have. I've always wanted to own that boat."

Gary returns from the shed, empty-handed now except for some peanuts, which he chews meditatively. He and Curtsinger resume their conversation. They talk of herring. They talk of herring spawn. They talk of the scientist Bill knows, the man who is studying herring spawn. "Did you read that article in the paper?" Gary asks. "Some scientist was saying we should switch from lobster to herring." He shakes his head, incredulous. "Now how are we going to do that? Herring is an endangered species, almost. I don't know what goes through these people's heads. She was a woman, this scientist. From Tufts."

Bill nods. He, too, is often puzzled by scientists and has some good stories to tell about them. He chooses not to tell them now. Instead he asks Gary how the lobstering has been in the months of his absence.

"Pretty good. Spring was terrific, the best in years, but then we had that storm in April—not so good after. These things even out."

Bill likes this last bit of philosophy, this fisherman's fatalism, but with Gary he does not let on. Instead, he begins kidding his friend. Turning to me, Bill says, "You know, fishermen see a lot out there. Gary sees whales. 'Bill, I see whales out there, jumping around. What are they doing, Bill, mating?' Because that's all Gary has on his mind."

Gary laughs and does not deny it. He eats another peanut. "So," he asks, "where did you go this summer?"

"Alaska."

"Still chasing the poor wolves around?"

"No." For an instant Bill hesitates. "Walruses."

Gary grins and shakes his head. Dismissing Bill and walruses—that whole world—with a wave of his hand, he begins descending the pier ladder to his boat. Partway down he pauses, his foot lingering on a rung. "What do they do—call you when they need you?"

"Yep."

Gary rolls his eyes. "Why was I born a lobsterman?" he asks the ocean. With that he disappears entirely.

In Maine there is a certain amount of this friendly head-shaking over Bill's profession, and it bothers him a bit. He believes that Maine friends like Gary have an imperfect idea of his life in the field. Most of them are firmly rooted in Maine granite and seldom stray far. They think his career is a lark. They don't know about the hard work and the disappointment. Sometimes he wishes they did.

Walruses, Chukchi Sea

Black-browed albatross and dusky dolphin

4. Sharks

OR THE MOMENT the Roaring Forties had ceased to roar. The sky above Golfo San José was clear, the water calm, the dolphins plentiful. Bill Curtsinger, full of anticipation, grabbed his wetsuit and collected his fins.

Bill always wears a wetsuit, even in the tropics. In warm waters he uses a one-eighth-inch suit, partly as protection against fire corals, hydroids, and all the other stinging organisms of tropical seas; partly because after hours in it, even warm water gets cold; and partly because a wetsuit feels familiar. Here in Argentina he wore a quarter-inch suit. Undressing to put it on, he revealed briefly an old wound on his shoulder. The scar covered one side of the shoulder, a marbling of surface tissues. Five years old now, it was no longer angry red, just indignant. On his left hand was a second scar. It began near the heartline of his palm, angled toward the base of his little finger, then ran, thin and white, most of the way up that digit. He received both injuries at West Fayu Atoll of the Caroline Islands, in two separate passes by a gray reef shark.

Reaching back for the hood of the wetsuit, he tugged it on. Immediately he looked older. The hood crimped him around the eyes, accentuating the wrinkles there. He pulled on his face mask and adjusted it, and with that he changed appearance entirely. The mask distorted his upper lip and altered his voice. He looked like *someone* you knew, but it was someone other than Curtsinger. His voice became nasal, less pleasant than before. Bora had observed this transformation often, of course. He knew both Curtsingers well and was not alarmed.

Seizing his camera, the Jekyll-Curtsinger went over the side. Again he found himself in the heart of the anchovy-dolphin storm, but this time the storm was different.

"In the beginning, I was hot on this cylinder business," he says. "But now there was no cylinder—the fish were all spread out. The cylinder was only part of it. It was more complex than I thought."

Again walls of schooling fish sprinted past him, again the birds were busy with the anchovies at the top of the school, again the densest aggregation of surface birds marked the fastest underwater action, but this time the dolphins had not rolled the school into a cylinder. On several occasions the school was lenticular, and Bill watched the dolphins, four or five at a time, holding themselves vertically in the water and chomping anchovies, their heads gone inside the haze of the school, like politicians in a smoke-filled room. Today he noticed that some dolphins seemed to be herders, some feeders. He tried to keep his impressions straight while he worried about exposure and maneuvered to get in better position. He wished that Bora, above in the Zodiac, were taking notes on the surface behavior of the dolphins and the birds. Later they could correlate the activity above with that below. He cursed Bora, *lazy Bora,* but he was too busy to put much venom in it.

Fortunately for Bill's sensibilities, the speed and chaos around him were silent. The only noises were the entry splashes of the birds, and occasionally the heavy, plunging reëntry of the dolphins. The dolphins were shouting over their intercoms, surely, but at a frequency too high for him to hear.

On the surface, when he was reloading his camera in Bloater between dives, or when the boat was chasing after the chase, he saw the most exuberant surface antics of all!

his time in Argentina. Dolphins rode the bow and breached to port and starboard. There must have been, he guessed, twenty different styles of breaching. Some dolphins jumped high and did end-over-ends. Some came out rolling. Some fell back headfirst, some flukes first. Duskies are the most acrobatic dolphins he has ever seen. Bora reported having spotted a penis during one breach, and later Bill watched a pair of dolphins breach several times together. For the first time, it occurred to Bill that breaching might sometimes be part of a mating ritual.

They could have been jumping, too, to rid themselves of parasites. They may have been jumping for joy. They may have jumped for the pleasure of full stomachs, or pleasure in the speed of the chase, or pleasure at the miracle of sonic sensation.

Or maybe they were jumping for quiet.

Perhaps it happens like this: A dolphin leaves off its herding and accelerates toward the silvery surface. With a few powerful undulations of its flukes, it reaches top speed, but it is imbedded still in a matrix of sound. The rapidfire clicks and queries of its companions; the tail-thrashing of the surface herders; the wash of the waves; the buzz of the Zodiac's outboard; the popping of shrimp; the frayed tuba notes of a whale, its song decaying now with distance; the mumble of screws of that Argentine destroyer maneuvering in the adjacent Golfo San Matias; along with a detritus of background noises no longer identifiable, all of these press in. The wind-textured, quicksilver underside of the ocean rushes up, to be obliterated suddenly by blue sky, and all the sea's chatter is left behind.

Perhaps for dolphins these are moments of suspended time. Maybe the dolphin soars into silence and hangs there. As it pirouettes in the thinness of air, its eye meets the unfiltered sun and stops way down. The spray scatters from its flanks, the droplets deploying themselves in space like smaller suns. At zenith the dolphin floats in solitude. All the subtle pressures that define its world, all the high-pitched conversation that unifies its tribe, all the hydrodynamics responsible for the evolution of its shape, along with most pleasures of the flesh, fall away. The sonic oscillations in the oil of its melon and jawbone even out, like those lines traced by a vital-sign machine when life has departed. The dolphin sails as pure mind into the bright ether of a temporary delphinid nirvana.

Then time resumes its normal pace. Gravity asserts itself—a sensation a dolphin knows only in air. The dolphin suddenly has weight. The ocean rushes up fast—blue on this side—and is obliterated in a white plunge of bubbles. The chatter commences again; the effervescence of the bubbles, the clicks and queries of the tribe, the change

in pitch as Bora throttles down the outboard, the underwater bark of a sea-lion bull patrolling his harem at Los Conos, a low groaning of mysterious origin, the clop of an albatross beak as it misses an anchovy, the basso profundo refrain of the whale song, the heavy sibilance of the surf on the beach.

Bill, underwater about six or seven miles from shore, was looking through the viewfinder of his Nikon's twenty-four millimeter lens, taking pictures, when he noticed something odd in a dolphin on the far side of the anchovy school.

Anyone reviewing that roll of film, on a light table, while warm and dry, relives some of Bill's emotion, and does the same double-take. The frames preceding the crucial one are full of action—fish scattering from the point of attack, dolphins careening, beetle-browed albatrosses glaring at the camera, cormorants slanting downward with necks extended, other cormorants rising, hollow boned and buoyant, their necks telescoped now, beaks pointed at the surface. In perusing all this arrested tumult, it is easy to pass the crucial frame without noticing, just as Bill nearly passed it in real life. The odd dolphin in the photograph is big, but, poised between camera and sun, its image is hazy, and the head is lost in the dazzle. Convergent evolution has carved its anomalous dorsal fin into a blade much like the dolphin's, and its flanks are similarly powerful and sleek. At the same time there is a world of difference, and you wonder how you almost missed it. The differences are hard to describe, having to do with curves and fullnesses. The strange dolphin is leaner and longer. Its caudal fin is very different, vertical where a dolphin's is horizontal.

"The shark was gulping whole mouthfuls of fish," says Bill. "That's what gave me notice. The mouth was open. You never see a dolphin's mouth open when it's feeding —or practically never. A dolphin always seems to take a single fish in front of him."

Five years before, snorkeling in fifteen feet of water on the lagoon bottom at West Fayu Atoll, Bill had been ascending, turning in a slow spiral to keep an eye on his surroundings, when he saw the blur of the reef shark, a gray torpedo aimed at his head. There had been time only to throw up his hand and turn his face aside.

Now, when this Argentine shark showed interest in him, he rose to the surface, spit out his snorkel, shouted, "Bora, shark!" then swam to Bloater and hauled himself in. The feeding frenzy was moving away. He returned almost instantly to the water. Gripping Bloater's side, he watched the shark pass directly beneath, and he held the

Dusky dolphin

camera toward it, his arm extended, keeping the heavy metal housing between them. The shark's eye rotated to watch the man, then its long shape vanished. Bill didn't know the species. The color, he decided, had been "greeny-bronzy-brown"—a white tip's coloration—and the eyes looked like a white-tip's. The shark seemed thin. The snout was rounded. He could not remember the tail. He thought, correctly, that he might have a photograph, because he recalled shooting in that direction before he realized the shark.

The dolphins had passed on. Bill hauled out again, frustrated.

"It was the best situation, beyond a shadow of a doubt, that we had had in two months in Argentina," he says. "The calmest day, the fastest water. Everything seemed sort of stationary. The fish weren't moving much. It was perfect. Perfect light, and a flat, dead-ass calm. It was too good to be true."

The West Fayu shark, hitting Bill in its first pass, had torn his hand and ripped off his mask and snorkel. Reaching the surface, he had screamed.

Now, as he sat in Bloater, he silently maligned himself. If he had kept cool, he thought, maybe the shark would have ignored him. It was busy with the anchovies, after all. If only he hadn't been alone in the water, if only he had known the species of shark, and thus what to expect from it. His fright ebbed, and he felt foolish. He was left with an acute sense of his tininess, inefficiency, and vulnerabil-

ity in the water. His illusion of being an honorary dolphin had vanished. The dolphins had shown not the slightest alarm at the presence of the shark.

On February 20, after two weeks of bad weather, the gulf calmed enough for Bloater to go out again. They saw no dolphins, but offshore they encountered a sick yearling penguin. It was paddling feebly, too weak to protest when they lifted it aboard. Bora decided they should adopt the penguin and he named it Ralph. They brought Ralph ashore, netted some anchovies, and force-fed him. (Or her. "It's almost impossible to sex a penguin," says Bill. "You have to do minor surgery practically to find out.") Bora, having rescued Ralph and named him, washed his hands of the matter. Bora has the kind of mind that daily requires new entertainment. It was left to Bill and Kate to feed Ralph, and Bill found he liked the job. He is a man full of sentiment for certain people—for Marshall Alexander, a fisherman back in Maine, for Chuck Nicklin, an underwater film-maker from San Diego, for Bora, for Bobby "Bloater" Flynn and his wife Alice, who live on Long Island—and Ralph now joined that select company.

"Ralph adds a new dimension to our lives here," he wrote. "Rising early to net him some fish, an easy ten minute task. He is very sick—extremely weak and emaciated. The first full day here at camp I wasn't at all optimistic about his chances, but now, three days later, he is standing erect under his own power—a wobbly stance at best, but two days ago he could barely lift his head from the floor. We have been feeding him two or three times a day. Yesterday we gave him a little tetracycline and today, inside a fish, we placed a One-a-day brand multiple vitamin. He has eaten so far today 42 anchovy. Yesterday about 30 and the day before maybe 18. He is out on the porch now with Kate and me. Bora is at his desk listening to the Paul Winter Consort.

"We are having a lovely time here, enjoying our closeness with the sea, the desert, the bird fauna. The sound of oystercatchers down the beach. The gulls in their huddle, lifting off to feed as the intertidal zone is exposed on the falling tide. The cormorants and grebes fishing offshore for the same anchovies that we net for Ralph. The penguins that sit down the beach. There are three now, one adult and two juveniles.

"Ralph has just stood up again for a stretch. He is really doing much better and we're really pulling for him. The three penguins down the beach are so fat and fluffy and poor Ralph is a bag of bones. The beach here has a penguin carcass at every 50 paces or so. I have not thought much about them. My natural-history consciousness began in a penguin rookery in Antarctica, watching skuas snatch eggs and chicks, and eating whatever was left of mature birds after leopard seals finished tearing them apart. But Ralph, old weak emaciated bag of bones Ralph, swims into our lives and one can't help but think about all the carcasses lying on the beach and Ralph would have been one in a day or so—still could be for that matter, even after we fatten him up and direct him down the beach to be with his own kind. Maybe it just isn't written in the stars for Ralph to make it, although I keep thinking that once he is back in good physical condition again he has, so to speak, a new lease on life. I just hope old Ralph, who isn't old at all, actually this summer's babe, I just hope poor old Ralph can pay the rent.''

Before turning in that night, Bill looked in on Ralph one last time. As always with Ralph, Bill made penguin noises, a couple of strangled squawks. This time Ralph answered, a single note, the first sound they had heard from him.

''Toward the end it was just so good,'' Bill says, of the dolphin feeding frenzies. ''Each time seemed better than the others. To have *seen* it, to have been in the middle of it all. I never got tired of it.

''Well, I suppose I did get tired after eleven, twelve hours in the water. It's usually when nothing is going on, when all you see in the water is scales, then's when you're feeling tired. The time I feel how tired I am is when I drag my body over the side into the boat. You think, 'How many more times can I pull myself out of the water?' Sometimes after real long swims, when the dolphins were just out of range and I was trying to catch them, I would just stop in the water and call for the boat. It was hopeless trying to keep up. But if something was happening in the water, I wouldn't feel tired. The excitement carries you.''

One clear morning, Bill and Bora sighted dolphins feeding offshore and they motored out, leaving Ralph and Kate on the beach. They joined the dolphins, and Bill spent one tank of air getting what were, he thought, good pictures. Then he realized he had left the lens cap on. It was the only time in his career he has made that mistake. They sped ashore for a fresh tank and soon were back among the dolphins again.

Bill swam toward a small, dense school of anchovies.

Dusky dolphin and gulls

Close behind him swam Bora, towing Bloater and watching his partner photograph the dolphins slicing through the school. Bill noticed through his viewfinder that no birds were strafing the upper corners of his frame. They were frightened of the boat, he guessed. He wanted birds in the picture, so he asked Bora not to follow so close.

Bora dutifully fell behind. Moments later, twenty feet below the surface, Bill was watching through his viewfinder as waves of dolphins streaked by, when in the midst of one wave came a shark. It was the same unknown species he had seen before.

"The shark was swimming along with them just as if he thought he was a dolphin. He came over to me absolutely without hesitation. 'Without hesitation' is an understatement. There was no time to load."

Bill switched his camera from his right hand to his left, grabbed his empty bang stick, then got it down on line with the shark, and he thought, *Here we go again.*

On West Fayu Atoll, on the day of *that* shark, Bill had been wearing his Jetfins. It was the first time he had used the big fins in the Pacific, and he is glad he chose them, on that day of all days, for Jetfins are much faster than the little fins he commonly wore. "I was screaming hysterically," he recalls, "but swimming my ass off." He swam on his back toward the boat. Each time he dipped his hand in the water, he struck up a cloud of blood. He noticed this, but there was nothing to be done. If his hand was hurting him, he was too scared to know. A crewman, Otey, had jumped into the dinghy and was rowing furiously toward him. The others, running to the rail of the trimaran, saw Curtsinger, water boiling from his fins, steam toward them. While the men watched from deck, the fin moved in, and the shark raked his shoulder.

A bang stick, or powerhead, is a simple affair, a high-powered cartridge on the end of a stick. In Argentina, Bill's stick was empty because that is the acceptable way to carry bang sticks. Kept loaded for any length of time, the stick would blow off a diver's leg or some other part of his anatomy the moment he was clumsy or forgetful. Bill used a Sea-way "fast-load" powerhead, which employs a .38 caliber cartridge with a casing specially modified for use underwater. On striking the shark's nose, the cartridge is pushed into a firing pin and explodes, excavating a great hole in the shark and ejecting itself. Bill carried his cartridges tucked in a pocket on the right thigh of his wetsuit. He was encumbered by his camera, and there was no easy way to reach across for the cartridge, then load the stick with his left hand. This moment of awkwardness, with Argentine shark of unknown identity approaching, was the genesis of a new system. Afterward, Bill and Bora would twist rubberbands around the tips of their sticks and hold the cartridges there.

The shark put its nose to the bangstick. Feeling the hard steel, it turned tail and departed as quickly as it had come. It ceased playing shark and returned to pretending it was a dolphin. Bill turned and saw Bora on his way down with the long bangstick.

The incident had become one of those fairly routine in the life of a diver. (Curious shark encounters steel tip of rod or powerhead and, no longer curious, departs with flick of tail.) But for Bill, no shark encounter will ever again feel quite routine. "He's a little more leery of sharks than most divers," says Bora. "I'm sure it's always in the back of his mind—that one of these days he'll be fish shit."

Aboard the trimaran in West Fayu Atoll was a doctor, David Lewis, a competent and adventurous man who once tried to sail solo around Antarctica. When the dinghy brought Bill in, Dr. Lewis asked Bill to flex his fingers. Bill was able to do so, which meant that no tendon had been severed, though tendon sheaths had been exposed. Of the second wound, Dr. Lewis says, "the shark's teeth missed the major vessels in the neck by a hair's breadth."

There is a photograph of Bill taken shortly after his narrow salvation. In it he sits slackly against a bulkhead of the trimaran, his legs sprawled in front of him, his arm and shoulder wrapped in dirty bandages. Beardless then, he looks younger. His smile is exceedingly wan.

"Ralph is dead," Bill wrote in his journal. "His lifeless carcass is drifting across the bay or washed ashore somewhere looking like all the others. I miss Ralph. I think of him and the visible signs of progressively good health he gave us now and then; and I miss caring for him—going down to the sea each morning to net some fish; looking in on him in his room.

"I threw his still warm body as far out onto the water as I could without making the act too unceremonious. Kate, on seeing his stiff webbed feet erect like little sails said something like: 'O Christ.' I wanted to give Ralph a good start on his journey. I didn't want him drifting up on our shore. He seemed well the day he died. He ate 20 fish in the morning with what appeared to be gusto. I cried after throwing Ralph out. I walked north along the beach with Ralph drifting in the same direction but at a much slower speed. I turned back to watch him drift along several times. Good-bye Ralph. It was nice knowing you. I wish you could have made it. I wish we could have fattened you up to look like your buddies down the beach."

5. The Creature from Kennebunkport Marsh

LEAVING the Cape Porpoise pier, Bill and I step through the tangle of warp and lobster pots and return to his car.

The Volvo is an off-white 1964 model. The license plate says "WHALES." Special plates in Maine, personalized or cetaceanized, cost ten dollars. Bill was the first in the state to think of WHALES and send in the fee. He and Kate have a newer car, a Pinto stationwagon, but he prefers the Volvo. He is affectionate about the old car and refers to it always as "Whales," never as "the Volvo." Today the interior of Whales is messy. A layer of junk mail, pamphlets, roadmaps, and old letters insulates the floor.

He turns the key. Whales spouts a double puff of oil smoke, then the engine catches and we are underway.

Bill resumes his navigation of the lanes of York County. They are pleasant lanes. The towns of this coast are all Stuart Little towns, each one the loveliest in the world. They are composed of equal parts town and country. The stark Maine architecture is white-painted, usually, and two-storied. Wood piles are growing with the approach of winter. Autumn has passed its peak, and its scarlets and yellows are fading.

In the village of Kennebunkport, Bill stops again. He parks the Volvo and leads the way up wooden stairs to a small bookstore, "Kennebunk Book Port." A sign in the window announces that shoes and shirts are *not* required inside. We enter and browse. The shelves, stocked for the now-vanished summer crowd, are heavy on books about Maine, especially picture books, to which Bill gravitates. He selects *The Night Sky Book,* "a guidebook to the Northern stars for kids and grown-ups," and takes it to the counter. The store owner, figuring the tax, smiles at him.

"Well, Bill, do you have any books in the works?"

Bill glances at me uneasily. Is the man clairvoyant? Bill has never done a book before. We have only just begun our collaboration on this one. He answers that yes, as a matter of fact, he is thinking of a book, a book on sea mammals.

The owner wears a graying beard, neatly trimmed, and

a soft, white, immaculate sweater. His enunciation is mincing, his manner gossipy as we discuss, briefly, books and publishers. Curtsinger is reserved. He is not so easy now as he was with the lobsterman. The photographer is a former Navy diver. He speaks the language of regular men. He is most comfortable in the company of people who live by the wit of their hands.

We walk outside, and the door shuts behind us. "I didn't want to get into a big discussion about the book," he explains. "I like to keep a low profile around here."

Whales blows once more, and we start home to Biddeford Pool.

"The Pool," as residents call it, is part of a coastal annex to the town of Biddeford, which itself is a satellite of Portland. The Pool has three hundred residents in winter, more than a thousand in summer. A single dead-end road leads in. Its two lanes run eastward from Biddeford nearly to the coast, then turn north into a straight, mile-long stretch called "The Stretch." On one side of the Stretch is a low dune ridge covered with beach grass. In the grass at regular intervals stands a row of houses, most of them occupied only in summer. On the other side is the pool itself, a tidal basin rimmed by salt marsh. Sometimes, when high wind and high tide coincide, the Atlantic flows in sheets over the road and into the pool, but normally the pool fills and empties less dramatically, through a narrow gut that opens onto Winter Harbor to the north. Bill and Kate live at the end of the Stretch, where the road departs its straight course and begins ramifying to serve their neighbors.

Whales enters the Stretch. To our left the green-gold, soft yet spiky horizon of the salt marsh races past. It was marsh like this that first drew Bill Curtsinger to Maine, five years ago, after *National Geographic* assigned him a salt-marsh story.

His method was simple. He had someone drive him to Goose Rocks, near the marsh entrance, just as the tide was beginning to enter. The marsh sucked him like a microbe into its arteries. "You can't swim against the current," he says. "You're being swept into the marsh. You're not just photographing it—you're coming in with all the nutrients. You aren't a part of the ecosystem, or anything, but you really sort of are." He wore a black, quarter-inch wetsuit. Fins were unnecessary. He was propelled instead by moon-pull, driven by the tide from the marsh's arteries to its capillaries. The widest of the arteries were twenty yards across. The narrowest of the capillaries were three feet in width. He drifted for hours, hardly moving. He was liberated from volition. He might

have been a Portuguese man of war, except that his tissues had achieved a higher level of organization. He might have been a basking turtle, except that he was wide awake. The water was never more than ten feet deep. It averaged about five. Shrimp scooted away beneath him. Flounders fed, mussels filtered, snails foraged. The marsh was inhabited by the species that live in any East Coast salt marsh, but here in Maine the water was clear and he could get pictures. He remembers best a certain snail, a periwinkle, *Littorina littorea.* Lying at the edge of a plain of marsh grass, Bill watched the periwinkle climb a single blade, maintaining a millimeter lead over the rising tide. When it reached the top, the blade bent nearly double with the weight. Bill was rapt. This was only a small mollusk inches in front of his face mask, yet it was as momentous, as it solved its tiny problem, as any of the great whales. Had Bill straightened, he could have stood on muddy bottom, yet he was as excited as if an abyssal trench six miles deep had yawned beneath.

The idea was so natural, its execution so effortless, that no one had thought of it before. "It was just the nicest thing I've ever done," he says. "The only problem with traveling so light was I couldn't reload. I had just the one roll, thirty-six chances." He slipped through the marsh as disciplined as a Zen archer, or as the young Daniel Boone sent into the woods with a single bullet.

In one bend of one channel, the water was relatively deep, and the bottom was alive with flounder and mussels. Bill worked it like a rich vein. He snorkeled on the surface, picking his subjects, then made heroic ten-foot dives. Glancing up after one dive, he saw a man and his dog on the sand bank above, looking down. He had no idea how long they had been watching him. He was struck by how closely the dog, an afghan, resembled its master. The man was Hale Whitehouse, and this was their first meeting. Hale was clam warden for Kennebunkport and these clam flats were his domain. It was illegal for non-residents to take Kennebunkport clams, and Hale, Bill is certain, suspected him of having dreamed up a new clam-poaching wrinkle.

"Hi," said Bill.

"Hi," answered the clam warden. It was the beginning of a long and laconic acquaintance.

Bill's girlfriend of those days, Jane, lived on the marsh. When he had used the last of his thirty-six chances, he simply stood up and emerged. He walked to Jane's place and knocked. She opened the door, and there on her porch he stood, black, rubbery, dripping, the Creature from Kennebunkport Marsh.

Huzza Porpoise . . . I call him thus, because he always swims in hilarious shoals, which upon the broad sea keep tossing themselves to heaven like caps in a Fourth-of-July crowd.

. . .

Their appearance is generally hailed with delight by the mariner. Full of fine spirits, they invariably come from the breezy billows to windward. They are the lads that always live before the wind. They are accounted a lucky omen. If you yourself can withstand three cheers at beholding these vivacious fish, then heaven help ye; the spirit of godly gamesomeness is not in ye.

—HERMAN MELVILLE

Spotted-dolphin calf, Hawaii

Spotted-dolphin calf leaping, Hawaii

When seen at a distance, the front part of the head of the young walrus, without tusks,
is not unlike the human face. As this animal is in the habit of rearing its head above the
water, to look at ships, and other passing objects, it is not at all improbable but that it
may have afforded foundation for some of the stories of Mermaids.
                                            —CAPTAIN WILLIAM SCORESBY

Walruses, Chukchi Sea

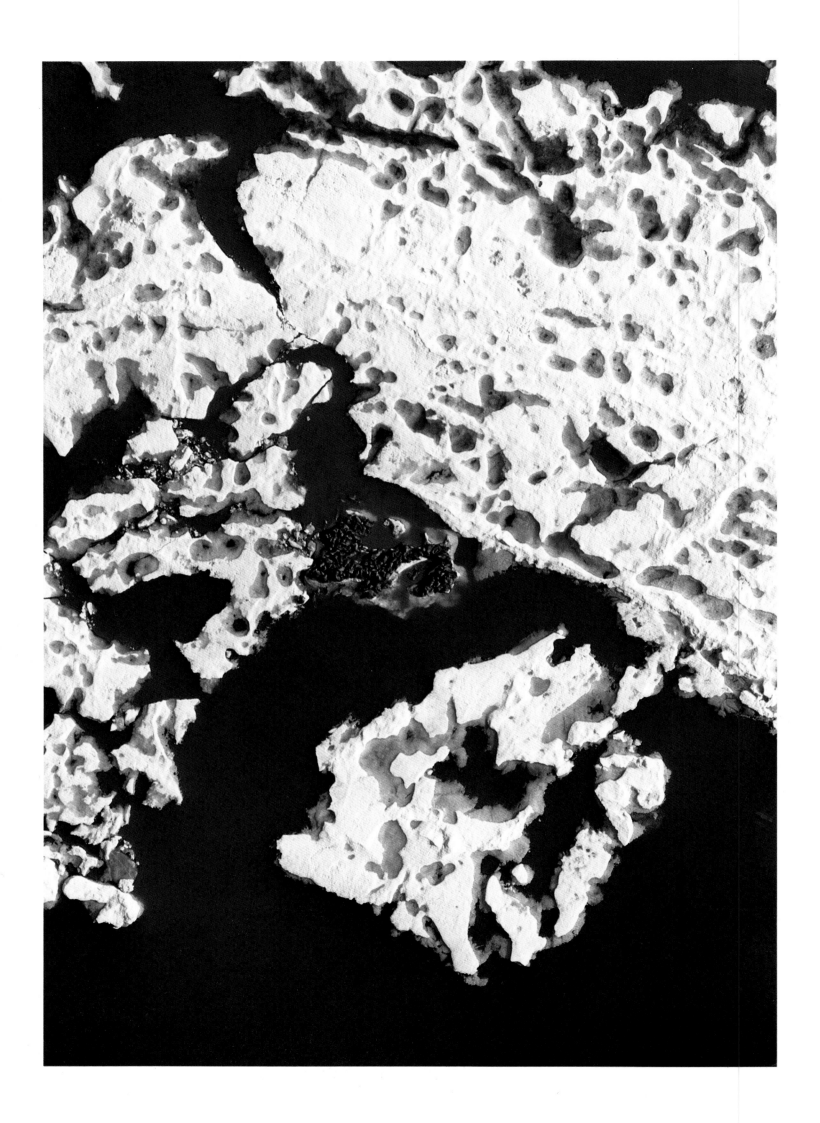

This formidable animal is, among quadrupeds, the sovereign of the arctic countries. He is powerful and courageous; savage and sagacious; apparently clumsy, yet not inactive. His senses are extremely acute, especially his sight and smell.
—WILLIAM SCORESBY

Walruses, Chukchi Sea

Polar bear eating walrus, Chukchi Sea

6. Antarctica

WHEN BILL CURTSINGER was young, his best friend was his gun. His interest in education departed him in high school. Teen-age society in suburban New Jersey was a jungle he chose not to enter. He found the pine barrens a more amenable wilderness. "I hunted mostly. I hunted everything. Deer, ducks. I was hardly without a gun for six years of my life." He fished, too, and found companionship in books, but his real buddy was the 12-gauge Remington pump, which he kept in immaculate condition and stored at his older sister's house.

"The first photograph I ever took was of a little box turtle in the pine barrens. I pressed the shutter and there was this little soft *click.* I couldn't believe it. I was used to this kaboom when you squeezed anything.

"I had a lot of trouble in my adolescent period. Fights and stuff. I wanted to do something with my life. I always suspected that I was going to do something, something good, although everything on the surface led you to believe the opposite. In high school I had one friend, a guidance counselor, Mary Keating. She believed in me, though I gave her every reason not to."

"Why did she believe?" I asked him once.

"I don't know. I don't know why. I believed in myself, but I don't know why that was, either."

With Mary Keating's help, Bill got into Northern Arizona University, where he received straight As and bought his first camera. The camera proved his undoing. On learning that Arizona State at Tempe had a photographic-art department, he transferred there. In the transfer he lost four units, was classified by the school a repeating freshman, and by the Selective Service as 1A. About to be drafted, he considered Canada. Instead he joined the Navy.

He began his professional career as a photographer by taking photo-triangulation pictures of gunnery exercises. Sitting on the tug that towed the target, he photographed the near splash of the shell while another sailor, sitting on the destroyer that was firing, photographed the far splash.

His first analogues for whales were giant Navy fighters. His Navy scrapbooks are filled with big silver planes, F-4s and A-6 Intruders, landing in dawn light on the decks of carriers. "As deadly a concept as those machines are, they intrigue me," he says. "They start at absolute zero and are airborne at one hundred twenty miles per hour in what—three seconds? I've never felt power like that." His tone, in recollecting that power, is full of an awe he would otherwise reserve for the power of flukes.

His first published photograph appeared in *The Virginia Pilot.* A shrimp boat off the coast had called the Navy to report a torpedo tangled in its net, and the Navy dispatched Bill along with the crew that was to disarm the thing. The torpedo proved to be a dredge pipe, but Bill's photo made the paper. "It was a dumpy little newspaper picture, but I got a lot of copies and sent them to my mother. I put it in plastic, even."

It was in the Navy that Bill became a diver. His naval strategy was to sign up for anything that looked interesting. He volunteered for dive school and spent a month learning about scuba gear and technique. He was now an underwater photographer. He worked with underwater demolition men, seal teams, frogmen.

He enjoyed the diving and the photography, but he hated the Navy. He had never realized how many stupid people existed in the world. The regimentation was dehumanizing. As a photographer he had a bit more freedom than most sailors, in that his officers never knew quite what to do with him. He became a genius at pretending to be busy. Ordered to participate in some make-work detail, he would demur, explaining that he had to clean his cameras. Much of his time in the service of his country was spent cleaning immaculate cameras.

In 1968 he volunteered for Antarctica.

It was a time when few sailors were interested in duty on the last continent, and the Navy was glad to send him. He was assigned to documenting the researches of the National Science Foundation, which the Navy supports logistically in Antarctica. The Antarctic quickly became his favorite place in the world. "It's a space that's almost impossible to describe," he describes it. "It's impossible even to discuss it. Its vastness . . . it happens to be the last

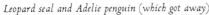
Leopard seal and Adelie penguin (which got away)

wild continent on Earth. It's beautiful and productive, but very hostile. It's almost totally a marine place. The Southern Ocean is what turned me on. The pack ice, the seals, the penguins.

"Spending time in a penguin rookery will get you. I've seen it happen again and again. Anyone who spends a lot of time in a penguin rookery, it happens to them. You're sitting there, with no place to go. You watch the whole social structure of the rookery; some chicks developing, some not, the skuas predatory on the chicks, the leopard seals predatory on the adults. You see the chicks going into the water. Not many are going to come back. It's just a heavy thing."

The vastness of the Antarctic, the drama of its rookeries, had an imprinting power in themselves. Bill brought to them, too, a willingness to be imprinted. His spirit was ready to expand into the vastness after its confinement on ships. Antarctica was beautiful first in itself, second as the landscape his young manhood was played against.

Rummaging recently in the attic at Biddeford Pool, he came upon his antarctic journal. It was written in his pinched hand on sheets from 3 x 5-inch notebooks. He skimmed a few pages. They embarrassed him, so he began declaiming passages aloud, disassociating himself by his overblown rendering from the youthful thoughts within. Then slowly, full of doubt about the wisdom of this, he handed the journal to me.

It is the journal of a young man ready to begin.

"Can't wait to get on the ice," he scribbled in New Zealand, in October 1968, on his way south. "Must get busy with my camera. I'm going to do a job no Navy photographer has ever done—that is, if I'm given a free reign. Now in the aircraft, one engine is beginning to turn. They say it's warm at McMurdo, fifteen below. Doesn't sound too bad, anyway. I wonder what lies before me?

Strange as it may seem, I shall see no more sunsets for four months or so. The beauty of the ice will make up for that, I'm sure. No more darkness except when I turn out the light myself."

The beauty of the ice, in fact, did not make up for the absence of sunsets. Antarctica greeted Bill grimly. The weather was bad, the sun did not shine, and he fell into a depression. For a week there are no entries in the journal. Then, ten days after his arrival, he wrote:

"Today I entered a world few men have seen, the waters under the ice. There were problems with my wetsuit and with the coldness, but I did it, I dove under the ice 130 feet and saw a vast array of animal life. Starfish, jellyfish, sponges. Had problems with my camera. Must rerig my holder for the flashbulbs. No pictures today, except of an unusual fish, but I was feeling my way, testing myself and my gear, and next time look out. Weight problem: First dive too buoyant, second dive sank like a rock. *Next time.* I can't wait for all the tomorrows that lie before me. I love you, Antarctica."

Among the things in the attic is a color photograph of Bill from those days. In it he stands in his wetsuit at the entrance to the new world—a hole in snow-covered sea ice. He's making an adjustment on his camera. He looks very Navy, in spite of himself, with a beard carefully trimmed to follow his jawline and a Navy haircut. He's leaner and younger. A cluster of blue flashbulbs dangles from his waist, like an egg cluster on an incubating frog. There is a white mountain in the distance, and the polar sun hangs low in a blue, blue antarctic sky.

"The diving was pretty hairy," Bill says now, "the hairiest I've ever done. The ice was eight feet thick. We wore quarter-inch wetsuits—that's all they had then. The wetsuits had zippers, and the cold would come in around them. Nowadays I don't think you could get anybody to

jump in those waters with quarter-inch suits. At depth, the neoprene is compressed to almost nothing, and the insulating quality is nil. I can't believe that I actually did it—that I got photographs in a suit like that, at depth. The work was all deep, usually in excess of a hundred feet. We always wore doubles, and the dives lasted an average of forty-five minutes. You're cold until your body warms the water in the wetsuit, then you're warm for a period, and then you're cold again. I was never really cold until I ran out of film, and then I was the coldest I've ever been. That's still true—if I'm underwater I'm not cold until the last frame. The second I'm out of film, I feel it.

"If the water had been fresh, it would have been frozen, but salt water freezes at a lower temperature. If you put a line over, ice would form on it. On the second stage of your regulator, there would be about an inch of ice. The things I've done since under the ice were a piece of cake."

On dives, Bill was the buddy of one or another of the scientists. He made instant friends with all of them and spent all the time he could in their company. They took him under wing, and he learned from them.

Paul Dayton, his principal mentor, was doing an ecological study of the benthos of McMurdo Sound. Dayton's method was to dynamite a hole in the ice over the zone he wanted to study. A snow-cat dragged out a plywood hut, which was set up over the hole. An oil heater was placed inside to keep the hole from freezing over at night. In the mornings Bill and the scientists would break through a half-inch pane of ice and dive.

"The ice is thick in Antarctica," Bill says. "In the Gulf of St. Lawrence, say, the ice is thinner and more greenish. In Antarctica the ice has a bluish cast. Underneath, there's much more of a deepy-blue darkish feeling. The light underwater depends on the amount of snow on the ice. If there's a lot of snow, very little light gets through. But the

water clarity was the greatest thing I've ever seen in my whole life. Before the plankton bloom, visibility was four to five hundred feet. I mean, you can't even *see* that far. Dark, but just so goddamn clear. After the plankton bloom, visibility is horrible."

Antarctica's benthic fauna has been isolated by cold circumpolar currents from the faunas of other continental shelves for forty million years. For all that time, the Antarctic Sea has had a constant physical regime, much like that of the deep sea, and its benthos has been colonized by a largely endemic collection of species with deep-sea affinities—or such is the impression of Paul Dayton and his colleagues. Bill watched Dayton and the others make transects along the bottom, collecting their benthic specimens. He levitated above as they left cages containing starfish on the bottom in growth-measuring experiments.

His strobe flashed. It illuminated a purple hydroid more beautiful, he thought, than any flower.

Leopard and Adelie (which didn't)

His strobe flashed. It lit the toadlike face of an ice fish. A ribbed, transparent dorsal fin ran the length of the fish's body, and its veins pulsed with antifreeze.

His strobe flashed. It lit a ghostly sea slug. The slug's tapering body, its delicate antennae, might have been carved in frosted glass. The slug had opacity and color only in the sprig of bright-yellow eggs it carried on its back. Its posterity was more substantial than its self.

His strobe flashed. It lit pale anemones, stalks imperceptibly salmon-colored and tentacles transparent. It lit white, broken bits of shell littering the gray sponge-mat. It lit brittle stars as colorless and slender-armed as those recorded by remote cameras on the floor of the abyss.

The antarctic bottom revealed by the sum of the flashes had a decrepit, devolutionary look. The strobe arrested motion, but in the dimness afterward Bill could see motion resuming, just barely. All the creatures moved excruciatingly slowly in the cold. They were life forms from the final days of a world whose sun was dying.

Some of the sea spiders were the size of plates. Some of the sponges were big enough for a diver to hide inside. "Polar giganticism," Bill explains. "The thing that's interesting is these things get huge, yet the growth rates are almost imperceptible. It's supposed to be several hundred years for a large volcano sponge."

In their collecting, the scientists stirred up clouds of sediment along the transects. Sometimes Bill got momentarily lost and disoriented inside the clouds, but rising twelve feet or so, he could get his head above the silt and see the ice hole he'd come down through. A shaft of light was always visible, plunging down into the blue. The antarctic sun shone twenty-four hours a day, and the pre-bloom waters were crystalline.

The ceiling of ice was dappled with luminous patches, large and small spots where the wind had swept away the snow. The men could see the straight track of light left by the snow-cat in its trips to the hut. A hundred feet under, they could hear the snow-cat returning, and sometimes they even heard a plane landing distantly on McMurdo's sea-ice runway. The man-made sounds filtered down to them through the constant, bizarre, otherworldly trilling of Weddell seals. Working under the ice, Bill and his friends became so accustomed to the otherworld that they no longer heard the trilling, and the bizarreness was lost on them.

Above, in the hut, jugs of hot water and galvanized tubs awaited the divers. The first man to pull himself through the hole was supposed to fill the tubs. On emerging, one at a time, the divers expectorated their regulators and exploded, as divers do, with excitement at what they had just seen. They coughed and shouted the questions and observations they had been unable to communicate underwater. Shaking and shivering, but still talking, they stripped off their wetsuits and eased themselves blissfully into the tubs. "Jesus, I can't even describe how it felt," Bill says. "I don't know if it was a good thing—it sort of drained your body. It was probably better just to dry off and get into your clothes. But it felt great.

"The floor of the hut was cold, but the air was hot from the oil heater. We always had some booze around. As an enlisted man I couldn't have liquor—only beer. But Paul was a scientist and he could have liquor, so he'd get it for me. I drank Tia Maria then—Jamaican coffee liqueur. If it was the last dive, we'd have a drink.

"We'd always just seen something exciting to talk about. Especially me, because everything was new to me. They tolerated endless questions from me. There was a lot of talk about women, too. When you're in Antarctica, there always is—there were no women in McMurdo then."

Someone had finagled a case of steaks, and they cooked these on the hut's small stove. They stored the steaks outside—in Antarctica there was no problem with spoilage.

In Bill's attic at Biddeford Pool, there is a black-and-white photo of the interior of the hut. It shows Paul Dayton and Bill sitting naked, side by side, in separate tubs. The fit is tight, and their legs are folded yoga-style under them, knees out of water. Clearly the hot water and the Tia Maria have begun to take effect. The excited conversation is over. Both men look tired and meditative. Each looks off in his own direction.

Excerpts from a young diver's journal:

Two dives again today. Everything went as smooth as hell. Again concentrating on Gordi and Paul running transects. Again the waters under the ice are as beautiful as ever. I love you, Antarctica.

* * *

I didn't get as cold as I usually do today. Must be getting used to it. The waters are as beautiful as ever. I'm going to hate to leave Dr. Paine, Gordi, Paul, Chuck, but I'll have to, and move along to some other phase of USARP study. How I love to dive here. Tried talking Paul into another dive tonight, but we're going to Cape Evans early tomorrow and we'll need full tanks. I wish that if I was ready to die I could be buried here beneath the ice.

* * *

Party tonight for Gordi's 101st dive through the ice. It was my 10th, and so equally a milestone for me. Steaks and champagne even while we sat in our tubs warming up.

In fine weather, seals prefer the ice to the water; and, when they find themselves dry and comfortable, have an aversion to take the water, and are sometimes easily caught.
—WILLIAM SCORESBY

Leopard seal eating penguin, Cape Crozier, Antarctica

Crabeater seal, Antarctic Peninsula

They are extremely watchful. Where a number are collected on the same piece of ice, one, if not more, is always looking round. And even a solitary seal is scarcely ever observed to allow a minute to pass without lifting its head.

—WILLIAM SCORESBY

Elephant seals, Antarctic Peninsula

Weddell seal, Deception Island, Antarctica

When I stand among these mightly Leviathan skeletons, skulls, tusks, jaws, ribs, and vertebrae, all characterized by partial resemblances to the existing breeds of sea-monsters; but at the same time bearing on the other hand similar affinities to the annihilated ante-chronical Leviathans, their incalculable seniors; I am, by a flood, borne back to that wondrous period, ere time itself can be said to have begun; for time began with man. Here Saturn's grey chaos rolls over me, and I obtain dim, shuddering glimpses into those Polar eternities; when wedged bastions of ice pressed hard upon what are now the Tropics; and in all the 25,000 miles of this world's circumference, not an inhabitable hand's breadth of land was visible. Then the whole world was the whale's; and, king of creation, he left his wake along the present lines of the Andes and the Himmalehs.

—HERMAN MELVILLE

* * *

Hallett Station. Penguins, beautiful Adelie penguins everywhere. The place is loaded now and they are still coming in droves, scooting along the ice on their bellies or waddling along in their curious way toward the nesting area. Hallett's beautiful. Large mountains surround us and icebergs, locked in by the seasonal ice, are at our doorstep. I sit out in the middle of the rookery and watch and photograph, and I can get very close and they are beautiful. I love it here, and out there by myself with only the penguins near me I am happy.

* * *

I'm penguin crazy. I talk to the birds and I occasionally catch myself looking around to see if anyone is within hearing distance, who after listening would consider me off my rocker.

* * *

One dive, 160 feet, 25 minutes. It was great to get back in the water once again. How I love it beneath the ice, where I am free like a gull to go up, down, around, gliding over the beautiful bottom trying to keep my mind off the cold and trying like hell to expose all thirty-six frames. Diving again tonight with Chuck. New hole now some fifty yards from the one I previously dove through. Just as spectactular, just as beautiful, just as cold. I love you, Antarctica.

* * *

Ran out of air at ninety feet today. Pulled my reserve,

or had Paul pull it, since he was available, and made it to the hole.

* * *

It's amazing how much faith I place upon my regulator. Yesterday when I was at 130 feet with Paul I thought of how I accept its performance without a thought. I just keep breathing, and it just keeps giving me air.

* * *

Zoomed around some playing 'Red Baron' with Chuck. It's such a neat feeling to be able to 'fly' underwater, turning somersaults and various other maneuvers. . . . Looks like another one-dive day again. Everyone seems pooped and for myself I think it's from sitting in the hot tubs for so long.

* * *

The deeper we got, the lighter and brighter the water was. Ice overhead is free of snow. Collected some hydroid sponges for Paul, a new nudibranch for Gordi. The damn hole is really invisible when down deep. I was really shocked as hell for a moment or two, looking for it unsuccessfully. Paul was below me some twenty feet and I could see that he was concerned about it. For a few seconds I was somewhat startled about its disappearance, and being my 49th dive this was the first time I have become greatly concerned and scared shitless.

* * *

I had the strangest feeling when Paul and Gordi got on

the plane. I hated like hell to see them go. But as they got on the plane, there was a moment when everyone started to rush a little to get aboard and get a good seat. I felt sorry for them. They were returning to the world of people, loads of people, in competition with each other for a lousy seat on a plane or on the subway. I felt lucky in a way, and also very sad to see them go.

*   *   *

Bill remembers the antarctic surf coming up one night, carving the ice foot, sawing through the shelf from which he had photographed yesterday, sending it seaward. He remembers Antarctica's dry valleys, guarded by enormous wind-carved rocks weathered into every form imaginable. "What an artist the wind is," he wrote in his journal. He remembers an Adelie chick being pecked to death by skuas. He held the chick in his hand for a moment, and it peeped at him for sympathy. Its entrails protruded and it had lost a lot of blood, but it did not seem to know it was dying. Dave, Bill's partner, killed the chick as painlessly as possible, and they left it to the skuas. Bill remembers the "dim, bluey blue" under the ice early in the year, when the snow was deepest on top, and he remembers the day, down deep, that his regulator made a sudden, peculiar noise, scaring him. He remembers a particular hole in his wetglove, and how cold his left hand got that day. He remembers how cold his hands *always* were, underwater in Antarctica. He remembers falling in love with *Hero*, the National Science Foundation's research vessel. He remember the whistle of the wind in *Hero*'s rigging; the confident, metallic rhythm of her engines; the occasional thud of an ice chunk hitting her bow and resounding through the wooden hull; the passing cliffs, rising nearly vertical and disappearing into the clouds, rendering *Hero* tiny and vulnerable as she steamed underneath; icebergs, big as fortresses, carved fantastically, the ship picking her way through the blue-white maze of them; the ice floes, dotted with seals that looked up briefly at *Hero*, then nodded off again; and *Hero*'s crew, real sailors, men to whom a ship meant as much, Bill realized, as a camera meant to him. He remembers wishing he could live down here, somehow, on an antarctic island, with a girl he loved, a girl who loved Antarctica. "The past six months have changed my life considerably, I know," he wrote, aboard *Hero*. "This beautiful continent, filled with so many sights and sounds and silence. A silence that creeps in on you and sweeps you away." He remembers crossing Bismarck Strait to Final Island, then French Passage and Penola Strait, and how drunk he got on that voyage, trading his photographs for two lousy bottles of Scotch, of which the visiting steward of the *Shackleton* drank at least half, and how the visiting

cook, later in the evening, made advances, and how he, Bill, said nothing but made threatening motions with his half-empty Scotch bottle, pleased at how quickly this discouraged the cook. He remembers how seasick he was the next day. He remembers *Hero*'s trawl coming up heavy with white-blooded antarctic fish, among them a brain-shaped sponge that he got to keep when nobody wanted it. He remembers the rough passage by the huddle of islands called the Waifs, and his roommate, a Chilean scientist, and how they lost their cookies together and how Bill wished he spoke Spanish better, because the Chilean was an expert on the antarctic benthos. He remembers Deception Island, and the ruins of the British base there, demolished by an eruption a week before, cigarette cartons and personal belongings still lying around, the ground warm underfoot, the fumes of hydrogen sulfide thick and choking when the wind turned; and later, down the coast, a zone of fumeroles, with steam escaping from vents all around, and pools of boiling water at the edge of the frigid sea, pools that floated with cooked krill, the whole scene misty and primeval and smelling like boiled shrimp. He remembers Antarctica's wandering albatrosses and sooty albatrosses, and giant petrels, and antarctic terns. He remembers euphausiids and copepods and ctenophores.

He remembers seals:

Another beautiful day at Hallett. Spent most of my day with scientists taking blood samples from seals. We found ten or so and two females with pups, plus a crabeater. Had my turn at putting the bag over the seal's head.

*   *   *

Went in a seal hole along a large crack in the ice. Lots of seals and the view from below was spectacular. The sun was shining and beautiful rays of light would reach down through the numerous holes towards the darkness below. The crack from underwater was like a large cave. Shot some of the seals underwater, and when at one point I poked my head up through a hole, there was a seal moving toward the hole about five feet away. He kept coming until he was some ten inches away from me, and there we both were. I made some seal noises and he seemed to be answering back, telling me to get out of the hole, for he was coming in. Finally I submerged and stood away from the hole to photograph him entering the water. As soon as he entered and saw us from below, he got up through the hole as if he had seen a ghost. Maybe his vision is less accurate out of water.

*   *   *

Today I saw a seal lying on the 'beach,' sleeping in the

sun and dreaming as we do. I know it was—I can tell. God, what do they dream? What thoughts of the past or the morrow enter and leave their minds as they sleep in the sunshine of a beautiful antarctic day?

*   *   *

Spent most of this beautiful Christmas Day at the water's edge. I just can't seem to stay away from the seal activity. I saw a great chase this afternoon and my feelings toward the leopard seal have changed considerably. A dramatic race for life and the penguin lost. The leopard, a good-sized beast who had a scar on his left lip, probably from an encounter with another of his kind, just outswam, outmaneuvered, and outguessed the Adelie, and Adelies are no slouch underwater.

*   *   *

The seals of the Antarctic were Bill Curtsinger's first marine mammals. The antarctic seals—the Weddell, crab-eater, elephant, leopard, and Ross—are the *only* mammals on that continent. The leopard was his favorite, and remains his favorite seal today. "I watched them so much," he explains. "I've seen leopard seals outswim penguins, and penguins move so fast you can barely follow them with your eye. Leopards crash through the ice chasing penguins.

One night it was real cold, and ice about an inch thick covered most of the sea. They just bashed right through. They're real obstinate and singleminded. All seals move with a serpentine quality, but leopards the most so. They move the most fluidly. They bend their bodies in great Us, making turns after penguins."

There was another super seal in Antarctica, impressive in a quieter way. Bill's acquaintance with *Leptnychotes weddelli*, the Weddell seal, began in Dr. Gerald Kooyman's "sub-ice observation platform," a windowed chamber next to a seal hole. From it, an observer would watch for a monitored seal rising to the surface and he would warn Kooyman that it was coming. Bill's thing with Weddell seals was not love at first sight.

"Well, here I am," he confided to his journal, "freezing my ass right off as I sit in Kooyman's stupid little observation chamber five feet or so beneath the ice. He obviously thinks that I came out here to help his little project along this evening, and because I am what I am, I haven't argued with him about it. Only a few Ektachromes I'll get out of this, and probably a cold. A terrible hate for seals is growing in me."

But the terrible hate did not last, either for Weddells or

for Dr. Kooyman. Bill liked Kooyman, who was a quiet, competent man, and he admired Kooyman's kind of science. Dr. Kooyman was learning the dive physiology of his Weddells not by strapping them to boards and immersing them in pressure tanks, but in more natural circumstances. He did not require his seals to die for science. His method was to find a region of ice that was free of cracks and holes, for he had to be sure his seal would return to the hole from which he released it, and not swim off somewhere else, like a defecting spy, with its expensive instrument package. Kooyman's spot had to be far from any possible exit, for Weddell seals are known to swim great distances under the ice shelf, and they must possess fine navigational equipment for finding cracks along the route. Natural seal holes were always within swimming distance of other seal holes, so Kooyman had to dynamite an artificial one. A hut was placed over the hole to warm Kooyman while he waited to lift the instrument package from the surfacing seal. The underwater observation chamber was a short distance away, and in it was someone like Bill, shanghaied and pressed into duty.

"He looks for victims," Bill says today. "He invites them out and puts them to work. It's smart of him. It's the only way he can do it. He has to have someone in that observation chamber to tell him when the seal is coming, so he can be ready.

"The seal comes straight up. All of a sudden, from nowhere. It doesn't waste time. It zeroes in on the hole and

Adelie penguins returning to the rookery, Cape Crozier

heads there in a very determined way. You don't have much time to warn him before the seal is there."

Wild seals were captured and taken to the hole for testing. Kooyman outfitted them with capillary manometer, depth-time recorder, ultrasonic depth transmitter, and Tsurumi-Seikikosaku maximum depth recorder. Most dives lasted less than five minutes and went no deeper than 100 meters. When a dive lasted fifteen minutes, though, the seal often went down 300 meters. The fastest rate of dive was 104 meters per minute; the fastest ascent 120 meters. The longest dive, recorded in an adult female, lasted 43 minutes 20 seconds. The *deepest* dive, by an old bull, was 600 meters. This is the record dive for a seal of any species. The Weddell is the champion diver of the pinnipeds.

Hydrostatic pressure in the sea increases at the rate of one atmosphere for each ten meters of depth. Dr. Kooyman's old bull, then, down in the darkness nearly 2000 feet beneath the surface, had borne sixty atmospheres on his back. Kooyman found it hard to believe that *Leptonychotes weddelli* could go much deeper than that, yet, as he would write later, "It is difficult to lay down dogmatic conclusions about diving limits without more knowledge of the behavior of tissues and membranes and of ion exchange at those great depths."

While Bill Curtsinger, bundled at his observation window, froze his ass off, a Weddell seal, down in the real cold, its form distorted by the enormous weight of water, its capabilities a mystery, made its determined way up toward him, a messenger from his future.

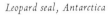

Leopard seal, Antarctica

7. Right Whales

BILL CURTSINGER's first cetacean was *Eubalaena australis,* the southern right whale. They met in Golfo San José in 1971. Bill, by now a contract photographer for *National Geographic,* was out in a Zodiac with Dr. Roger Payne. He rolled into the gulf's greenish water, and out of that green came the whale.

"It was a lot bigger than I ever expected," he remembers. "I'd never seen a whale before at all. The biggest thing I'd seen underwater was a seal. A right whale is such a big animal. It is just so big. Here was this hulk, this thing coming out of the gloom."

The hulk belonged to the suborder Mysticeti, a group named not for their mystery, though they possess plenty of that, but for their mouths. The name derives from *mystax,* the Greek for mustache, and it describes the fringed plates of baleen with which right whales, gray whales, and rorquals strain their food. The baleen does look something like a mustache, but an itchy and uncomfortable one, growing inside the lips. *Eubalaena australis* and the other members of the right-whale family *Balaenidae* have the longest baleen of any whales, with plates up to fourteen feet in length. The biggest of the family is the Greenland right whale, or bowhead. Smaller are the "black" right whales, of which there are several subspecies, among them the southern right. Smallest of the family are the pygmy rights, seldom longer than twenty feet. Except for the pygmy, the rights are the stockiest of whales, and among the largest. Herman Melville, for one, was not impressed, reserving his enthusiasm for "the great sperm whale, compared with which the Greenland whale is almost unworthy mentioning." He conceded, though, that, "in one respect this is the most venerable of leviathans, being the one first regularly hunted by man."

In the old days, the right whale was the "right" one to pursue, for it was slow, it yielded a lot of oil and baleen, and it floated after death. Among the mysticetes, it seems an early model. It lacks, along with speed, a dorsal fin and the accordian pleats in the throat that distinguish the rorquals, allowing those highly specialized whales, slender when at rest, to inflate to blimps when feeding. The right whale—dark, girthy, torpedo-shaped, with pectoral fins like paddles—is a model nearly obsolete. Its populations were the first to be decimated by whaling. Of the

southern right whale, it is unlikely that there are more than 1500 representatives left. The animals that visited Golfo San José to breed were relics of a race. From the cetacean point of view, the right whale has proved wrong.

Bill Curtsinger's first whale, a hulking emissary from a vanishing tribe—an emissary approximately the size of a freight car—approached Bill Curtsinger, a delegate from the tribe that had wiped it out. The whale stopped and shook its head threateningly.

"Roger had gone out of his way to assure us there was no danger," Bill says. "I took this to heart and never worried about a thing. So the first thing that happens is this whale puts on an aggressive display. It was the first time Roger had ever seen aggression, and the only time *I've* ever seen it, in a whale. Roger was horrified. It got semichaotic, with Roger yelling on the surface. I was in the water looking at it, *and it wasn't that bad.* It was definitely an aggressive motion, a side-to-side movement of the head, and on the surface you'd see this terrific frothing. But underwater it didn't look that bad.

"Roger Payne is a pretty neat guy, for a scientist. He's super bright, and witty, and tells a good story, and I like him a lot. I wish I had a mind like his. *But Roger never gets in the water.* He was removed from what was going on."

Bill was unfrightened by his first whales, but confused. In construction the right whale is perhaps the most peculiar of cetaceans, its features the most difficult to read. The head is enormous, with a lantern jaw. The eye is at the corner of the mouth. The line of the mouth curves steeply up and forward, so that when the whale, feeding, opens wide, its baleen mustache rises far above its eyes. The nostrils lie a hop, skip, and jump backward of the nose, and the whole visage is adorned with protuberant callosities.

At first glance, according to Melville, the right whale's head looks like a gigantic galliot-toed shoe. "But as you come nearer to this great head it begins to assume different aspects, according to your point of view. If you stand on its summit and look at these two *f*-shaped spout-holes, you would take the whole head for an enormous bass-viol, and these spiracles, the apertures in its sounding-board. Then, again, if you fix your eye upon this strange, crested, comb-like incrustation on top of the mass—this green, barnacled thing, which the Greenlanders call the 'crown' and the Southern fishers the 'bonnet' of the Right Whale; fixing your eyes solely on this, you would take the head for the trunk of some huge oak, with a bird's nest in its crotch. At any rate, when you watch those live crabs that nestle here on this bonnet, such an idea will be almost sure to occur to you.''

The aspects continued to change for Melville, and new metaphors continued to occur to him, though his whale was dead, hoisted into daylight at the side of his ship. Bill's whale was living. It was in constant, majestic motion, and he viewed it through green water. "It took a long time to make out bits and pieces of anatomy," he says.

Bill spent a month with the whales of Peninsula Valdés. That desert peninsula, to which he would return in six years to photograph dusky dolphins, became, after Antarctica, his favorite place in the world. His partner there, Chuck Nicklin, became one of his closest friends.

It was a wild and lonely coast, a thousand miles and twenty-five flat tires away from civilization. ("We drove down from Buenos Aires in two Renaults," he recalls. "Half of that thousand miles was gravel. We had fifteen flat tires and two broken windshields, if you can feature that. The tires just melted. When the Argentines passed going the other way, they would brace their windshields with their hands. They all did that—in case a stone hit. Someone had told them that it stops the vibration and saves the glass. We did it too. It didn't work. One second the windshield turns to ice, the next second it's in your lap. On the way back we had ten flat tires—twenty-five flats in all.") They lived in a motel in the one-horse town of Piramides, on the isthmus between Golfo San José to the north and Golfo Nuevo to the south. The motel beds were miniscule and the floors concrete. There was a ping-pong table, which provided their evening recreation. They ate breakfast early. A man at the motel packed them lunches.

From the cliffs above Golfo Nuevo, they would watch for whales. Seeing some, they would motor out in their Zodiac. Occasionally they worked in Golfo San José, joining Dr. Payne. More often they stayed in Golfo Nuevo, where they would not hinder Dr. Payne and science, and where science would not hinder them.

In stormy weather, they stayed in and watched from the clifftops. The whales, of course, stayed out.

When the Roaring Forties raise whitecaps in Argentina's gulfs, the breaching and lobtailing of the right whales increases. The whales beat the waves to make white water of their own. Dr. Payne thinks this may be a form of communication. Storms, he reasons, cause a lot of low-frequency wave noise underwater, and low frequencies are those at which whales exchange information. The slapping of flukes and the thunder of breaching might be ways of shouting, "Here I am!" The breaching and lobtailing is also, Dr. Payne suspects, a lot of fun. "The creatures that perform these acrobatics are so large," he has written, "so aloof from the normal torment and buffetings of this world, that they are, quite literally, playing with the storm." In moderate winds, one game was sailing. The whales raised their flukes above the water, presented them at right angles to the wind, and sailed shoreward. When they bumped bottom in the shallows, they circled upwind and sailed in once more.

When the wind ceased, Bill and Chuck went out again. In calm weather, the Argentine gulfs were the best places for whales that either man has ever visited. "It was a paradise," Bill says. "Chuck Nicklin and I were the first to photograph something like that. Compared with anything I've done on whales since, it was duck soup. It's harder now in Argentina, because people have harassed the whales."

The bottom at Golfo Nuevo was mossy in some places, sandy in others. The visibility underwater was usually good. Sometimes the whales swam back and forth in the same place, stirring up the bottom, but generally they were cooperative. "It was easier, even, than with humpbacks in Hawaii. In Argentina right whales are preoccupied with mating. You can get so close to those guys and they just don't care. Everywhere I've ever been since, I've wished that for just five minutes the whales would act like right whales. In Argentina everything was moving so slowly, in the middle of these courtship rites, that I was actually able to swim back to the Zodiac, reload, and swim out to them again. Time and time again, right whales turn around and just come back to look at you. Nobody else does that."

When a whale appeared, it was at first a dark looming in the green, a shadow in the water. The shadow grew larger. Making a course correction, it changed shape, then abruptly it was recognizably a whale. The whale's head passed, and the grapefruit-sized eye rotated to follow Bill. The great flank slid by him as dark and graffitoed as a subway pulling away from 125th Street. Bill, mildly buffeted but unharmed, was the commuter who had missed the train. As the flank passed he saw the scratches, the scars, the patterns of new and old skin. Old skin was black, new skin Navy gray, and the patches of color alternated like those in camouflage clothing. In part this was the handiwork of gulls. Earlier, on the surface, Bill had seen gulls walking along the head and altering the pattern, pulling

Right whale and Chuck Nicklin, Patagonia

The smile of a whale is a built-in feature with which it is endowed at birth and retains throughout life. A land creature may yawn and snarl and frown, may screw up its forehead and grow wrinkled in old age; the face of the whale stays round and firm—expressionless.
—Victor Scheffer

that Sea-beast
Leviathan, which God of all his works
Created hugest that swim th' Ocean stream.
　　　　　　　　　　—PARADISE LOST

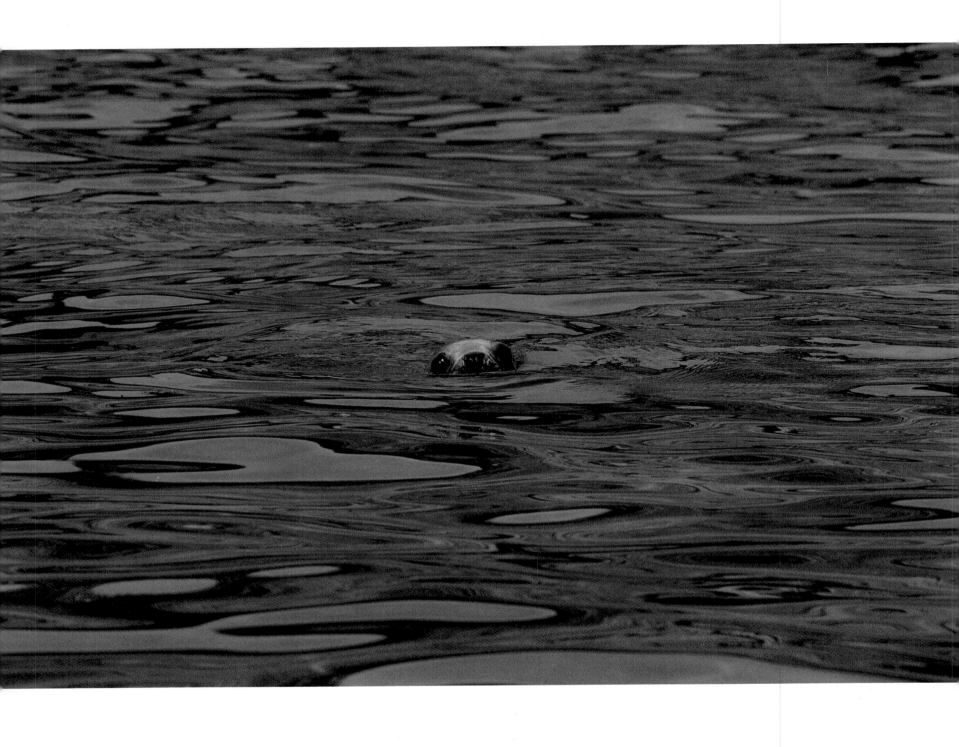

*They set out together across the Pacific, and Matkah showed Kotick how to sleep on his
back with his flippers tucked down by his side and his little nose just out of the water.
No cradle is so comfortable as the long, rocking swell of the Pacific.*
—RUDYARD KIPLING

Sea lion, Patagonia

Sea Lions, Patagonia

Every whale everywhere moves in a sea of total sound. From the moment of its birth until its final hour, day and night, it hears the endless orchestra of life around its massive frame. Silence is an unknown thing. . . . It feels the music too, for water presses firmly on its frame—a smooth continuous sounding board.
         —VICTOR SCHEFFER

off and eating strips of dead skin. The whales had liked it, or had seemed not to mind.

The whale passed silently. On rare occasions Bill heard deep grunts, and Dr. Payne's hydrophones sometimes recorded higher-pitched noises, but the right whale is never a singer like the humpback.

As the whale passed, Bill noticed tiny orange mites moving from one fold of skin to the next. The mites were most numerous on the rostrum and in the areas around the eyes.

Dr. Payne, wondering what they were, asked Bill once to pick one off, and he did. On examination it proved to be a young specimen of the adult white crab that inhabited the whale's callosities. "Right whales are born with these . . . warts," Bill explains. "Each whale has them in different shapes and places, like fingerprints. It's a rough, bumpy surface where the callosity will be. They're dark, both in calves and adults. The adult crabs are what turn them white." The advantages to the crabs of the symbiosis are obvious: they get a substrate to exist on, and a free ride, and food—krill that escapes the whale's sieve of baleen, or dead skin sloughing from the whale. The advantages to the whale are less apparent. Perhaps the crabs serve simply as cheap paint. "Roger thinks it's for marking—to give the callosities pigment. It helps the whales tell each other apart. It sure as hell helped Roger. If you're a scientist and you photograph a whale from the air, you've got a fingerprint."

One day a dead female washed ashore. She lay on the beach like a fallen black dirigible, her pectoral pointing to the sky. She began to swell in the sun, and blisters the size of canoes appeared on her skin. She was monumental and sad. A dry rivulet of milk ran from one teat into the sand. It was milk so rich—one-third fat, ten times the fat content of cow's milk—that it was tinged yellow, yet it would never fatten a calf. The whale's pigment of crabs was still alive. They moved about dolefully under the barnacle skyscrapers of their doomed cities. Bill stopped by for close-up photographs. Through his macro lens, the crabs looked healthy enough. The truth was they were dwellers on Vesuvius or Krakatoa. One afternoon, the whale exploded, and the next time Bill visited there were entrails all over the beach. "If you had been standing right there when it went off . . ." he speculates. Whale photography is full of unexpected hazards.

Underwater, the callosities slid past Bill, but never brushed him. It was a good thing they did not. Dr. Payne, who has watched right whales rub their faces across the flanks of rivals, believes the callosities are useful as sandpaper in fighting. An abrasive gesture intended merely to discourage another leviathan would have been, of course, intensely discouraging to Billy.

So, too, would have been a tap from the flukes.

"The whale slides right by," Bill says. "You watch the flukes coming. You're half expecting them to cut right through you."

Herman Melville, dissecting his whale with a flensing knife, wondered at the strength of the flukes. "The entire member seems a dense webbed bed of welded sinews," he wrote. "But as if this vast local power in the tendinous tail were not enough, the whole bulk of the leviathan is knit over with a warp and woof of muscular fibers and filaments, which passing on either side the loins and running down into the flukes, insensibly blend with them, and largely contribute to their might; so that in the tail the confluent measureless force of the whole whale seems concentrated to a point. Could annihilation occur to matter, this were the thing to do it.

"Nor does this—its amazing strength, at all tend to cripple the graceful flexion of its motions; where infantileness of ease undulates through a Titanism of power. On the contrary, those motions derive their most appalling beauty from it."

That appalling beauty, that Titanism of power, that measureless force of the whole whale concentrated to a point, was aimed now at Billy. That engine fit to annihilate matter was on line to annihilate our hero.

The killer whales that visited the Patagonian coast occasionally killed full-grown, half-ton sea lions by slapping them thirty and forty feet into the air with their flukes—flukes less mighty than those of the right whale.

"Harpooners have been struck dead by a single blow of a whale's tail, and other fishers have received dangerous wounds," wrote Captain William Scoresby, of the right whales he pursued in the Arctic early in the nineteenth century. He proceeded to fill his pages with examples: "On the 3rd of June 1811, a boat from the ship Resolution, commanded at the time by myself, put off in pursuit of a whale, and was rowed upon its back. At the moment that it was harpooned, it struck the side of the boat a violent blow with its tail, the shock of which threw the boat-steerer to some distance into the water. A repetition of the blow projected the harpooner and line manager in a similar way." Of a second whale, Scoresby wrote, "the boat was sunk by the shock; and, at the same time, whirled round with such velocity, that the boat-steerer was precipitated into the water, on the side next to the fish, and was accidently carried down to a considerable depth by its tail. After a minute or so, her erose to the surface of the water and was taken up."

Flukes, courting right whales

Of a third whale, Scoresby wrote, "A convulsive heave of the tail, which succeeded the wound, struck the boat at the stern; and by its reaction, projected the boat-steerer overboard. As the line in a moment dragged the boat beyond his reach, the crew threw some of their oars towards him for his support, one of which he fortunately seized. The ship and boats being at a considerable distance, and the fast-boat being rapidly drawn away from him, the harpooner cut the line, with the view of rescuing him from his dangerous situation. But no sooner was this act performed, than to their extreme mortification they discovered, that in consequence of some oars being thrown towards their floating companion, and others being broken or unshipped by the blow from the fish, one oar only remained; with which, owing to the force of the wind, they tried in vain to approach him. A considerable period elapsed, before any boat from the ship could afford him assistance, though the men strained every nerve for the purpose. At length, when they reached him, he was found with his arms stretched over an oar, almost deprived of sensation. On his arrival at the ship, he was in a deplorable condition. His clothes were frozen like mail, and his hair constituted a helmet of ice."

The flukes that caused all that damage in the nineteenth century now bore down on Bill.

"They never touched," he says. "I've been rocked by it, but never touched. The flukes lift up and over you."

He demonstrates. Making a wing of his hand, like a pilot in conversation, he shows how the flukes tilt up, sweep over and down again. At the same time he mimes himself, the diver, glancing up at the great shadow passing over.

"It misses you by four to six feet. Here is this animal, its eyeball forty-five feet past you, and yet it knows where you are the whole time."

Rocking in the wake of the whale was not an unpleasant sensation. Bill liked it. Some of the turbulence came, he judged, from the whale's bulk as it passed, but most of it rolled back from the flukes. He saw the turbulence before it hit him. "You could see the cavitation in the water coming off the flukes—a funnel, a dust devil, that comes off the tip of the fluke, a turbulence created by this mass of muscle. It's silvery and bright in the water. It doesn't move once the whale is by; it hangs there and then dissipates."

Bill had seen cavitation before, in the Navy, during submarine tests near Andros Island in the Bahamas. Underwater he had taken motion pictures of giant subs going by him at different speeds. Sooner or later he would record cavitation. The nautical engineers hated it when he did, for cavitations indicate inefficiencies in streamlining. The right whale had been endowed with such excesses of power, apparently, that the Nautical Engineer let the inefficiencies remain.

Sometimes the fluke action lifted sediment from the bottom, leaving it to hang in silty waves that marked the rhythm of the strokes. Sometimes Bill saw the flukes actually brush the bottom. When a whale was startled, the flukes pumped powerfully once, twice, and the whale disappeared in the green.

Bill has a rule about not touching his cetaceans, but occasionally in Argentina he broke it. "Every once in a while," he says, "you were presented with this fluke and it was just too inviting. One time I grabbed it."

"The tail," Captain Scoresby had written, of still another of his right whales, "was reared into the air, in a terrific attitude,—the impending blow was evident,—the harpooner, who was directly underneath, leaped overboard,—and the next moment the threatened stroke was impressed on the center of the boat, which buried it in the water. Happily no one was injured. The harpooner, who leaped overboard, escaped certain death by the act,—the tail having struck the very spot on which he stood. The effects of the blow were astonishing. The keel was broken,—the gunwales, and every plank, excepting two, were cut through."

"It was like a hard, smooth tire," says Bill. "The ride didn't last longer than a few seconds. I never did it again."

No one knows where the right whale comes from, when it arrives in July at Peninsula Valdés, and no one knows where it departs for in November. Dr. Payne's guess is that *Eubalaena australis* spends the southern summer harvesting krill around the Falkland Islands or South Georgia, but in surveys there he has yet to see a single specimen.

The whales come to the Argentine coast to bear their calves in the protected shallows. They court there, mate, and begin new calves. The calving occurs in September and October. The bulls, juveniles, and calfless females leave Argentina first, for wherever it is they go. The babies and their mothers are the last to leave.

One October day, a calf, in playful calisthenics that were training it for the migration it had yet to learn about, demonstrated Bill's contention about the importance of seeing your marine mammals underwater.

He and Chuck, out with Dr. Payne and several scientists in Zodiacs, came upon a baby whale, an infant the size of a delivery truck. "There was this calf zipping around," he says. "Whale calves love to play. They love to play in kelp. But they're babies, and they swim like babies. This one guy happened to be in the water in the path of a play sequence, and the calf hit him and bruised his rib. Roger yelled for us to get out of the water. We had to race away from this monster calf. I have a motor-drive sequence of the whole thing, underwater, and you can see that it wasn't intentional. Roger was visibly shaken and worried about us. Chuck and I couldn't understand it."

Bill has learned much of what he knows about right whales from Dr. Payne. His teacher misses things, Bill feels, in watching whales only from clifftops, Zodiacs, and kayaks. Bill thinks Roger should jump in the water.

In courtship, the performances were more ponderous and determined than the calf's, but, fortunately, in better control. Bill and Chuck swam unworried into the center of the dance. In the green boudoir of the gulf, they were the bedbugs. Around them colossal bodies twisted, rolled, stroked one another, mounted or evaded, unconcerned with the two insects that wandered among them. The insects, for their part, felt too insignificant to consider themselves voyeurs.

The whales mated belly to belly, with the males underneath. To avoid suitors a female would float at the surface, belly up, blowhole down, holding her breath. The bulls milled around, maneuvering for position, respiring easily and waiting for her to run out of air. When she rolled over for a breath, they dashed to be the first to align with her. The competition was mannerly, without much shoving, as it is with humans in respectable bars. A male technique was for the bull to lie directly under the female, belly up, holding his breath, for more than thirty minutes sometimes, and waiting for her to roll over and exhale. A female evasive technique was to hold her body perpendicular in the water with flukes in the air. For the male to align himself properly, he had to thrust his own flukes in the air, at which he instantly lost all maneuverability. There was no male counter to this female tactic. It was like asking a human male to make love on roller skates.

Occasionally the females failed in their evasions, or abandoned them, and Bill witnessed the act itself. The two whales stroked each other with their paddle-shaped pectorals as the male positioned himself beneath. The gray-pink penis seemed to have a life of its own, the tip searching about like a cobra.

When Bill and Chuck surfaced for air in the midst of the mating—they worked without tanks—their voices were crazy with excitement.

Yet it was the encounters with single animals—just Billy and a whale, that he seems to remember best.

"They turn back for *you*," he says. "It happened too many times for it to be anything else. They wonder, 'what's this thing hanging from my ceiling?'" Tilting its flukes sharply for a banking turn, the whale came back. The barnacled head, the black graffitoed wall, passed him once again.

"If you reached out to touch them, they'd pull the pectoral in, just the way they avoided you with the flukes. Not quick, but slowly. They're not frightened, but they don't want you touching them. The eye follows you. You can't read the mood. They're not expressive eyes. You only get to see one at a time, for one thing. They look right through you. Geez, it's just incredible. That one eye. That grapefruit eye."

The eye, in the right whale and other mysticetes, has been pushed backward by all the krill-straining equipment in front. It has migrated to the side of the head, where in defilade it escapes the full force of the sea as the whale swims forward. As a consequence the whale has no stereoscopic vision. Its depth perception of Billy depended on its movement toward him.

The eye was sturdily encapsulated to protect it from pressure in diving. The conjunctiva—the window in front of the lens—was thickened as protection against the batterings of the sea, and oiled against the salt. Because light in the ocean is dim, and because the ocean is full of things to watch out for, a whale's need for a bright picture supercedes its needs for sharpness, focusing ability, image size, color, and the ability to detect motion. The whale's pupil opens very wide. The lens is round, where in man and other daylight animals the lens is more conventionally lenticular. A round lens bends incoming light more sharply, projecting it on the retina in a small, bright image. Whales are huge animals but they see tiny. The surface of the whale retina is composed more of light-receiving rods than of color-receiving cones. In man the reverse is true. In whales, the retina is backed by the tapetum lucidum, a reflective layer of crystals that capture and amplify light. Had it been night, had Bill shined an underwater torch at his whale, the eye would have glowed, like a cat's on the edge of the highway.

The eye rotated up toward Bill and focused as best it could. A small, blurred Bill Curtsinger, his fair skin and blond hair dazzling, fell on the retinal screen within the armored orbit. *Eubalaena australis* saw a bright mote against a green heaven. Had the whale been Christian, and Nordic, and as full of wonder as the radiant being it now contemplated, it might have taken him for an angel. The whale was probably none of those things. It was certainly curious. Curiosity satisfied, it continued on its way.

Flukes, right whale

8. Slye's Hill

THE HOUSE in Biddeford Pool is a two-story frame building on an imperceptible rise of land that locals call, wishfully, Slye's Hill. On the spacious sun porch, a row of weathered chairs sits facing south, down the dune ridge. On one side is the Atlantic. On the other is the marsh, pool, and the pool's moored lobster boats. Bill and Kate do not sit in their chairs often. They don't live in their house, which is too large for two people and too costly to heat in winter. They rent it summers and dwell themselves, whenever they are home, in the loft of the barn next door.

The barn's horses are long gone, and the stalls are full now of shingles for kindling, yet the floorboards beneath retain the polish of hoofs. Split and stacked against one wall is a cord of oak. The people of Maine, unextravagant in other matters, burn oak as firewood. Against the split oak rests an axe. Embossing another wall are moose antlers. This might be any barn in Maine, except for the Scubapro Jetfins, the air tanks, the weight belts, the wetsuits of various thicknesses, the wetboots, the Healthways face masks, the Mako Engineering Model K-21 air compressor, the Scubapro air-tank backpacks and buoyancy compensators, the Johnson outboard, the Ocean-eye camera housing, the anchors, the waterproof aluminum camera cases, and all the other paraphernalia of Curtsinger's profession.

In one corner of the barn, a spiral stairway leads up to a trapdoor, which opens on the hayloft. The hay chutes remain, but the rest of the loft's interior is redone in rough-cut pine. The apartment is cozy, quickly heated by a small wood-burning stove.

Now, in October, each of the loft's windows frames a piece of autumn. The kitchen's dormer window holds the autumn blue of the pool. Above the blue is the tawny, autumnal horizon of the dry marsh. The bedroom window looks out on woodland, dark pitch pines and leafless poplars. The living-room window looks out past the edge of the woodland, down the dune ridge, over the dune grass to the ocean. In this window, on a tripod, is the spotting scope that once magnified dusky dolphins in Argentina. Here in Maine it enlarges the migrant birds that pause in Bill's trees.

The art on the pine walls has a marine-mammal motif. There is a print of whale flukes etched by Kate. There is a painting of a right whale by Larry Foster, an artist whom Bill much admires. A portrait of a leopard seal, taken by Bill on his second trip to Antarctica, when he returned to that continent for *National Geographic*, hangs above the door to the bedroom.

This leopard seal is a self portrait, very nearly. It came about strangely. Bill and his diving partner, who was a scientist, were one hundred and twenty feet beneath the surface of the Antarctic Ocean, collecting specimens along a transect line. The water was as cold as sea water can get, without freezing, and it was murky, with only ten-foot visibility. The strobe for Bill's camera had sprung a leak and was acting up, shorting out to flash randomly. Annoyed, he held the strobe above his head, trying to keep it level, which seemed to help. He watched the scientist working below him.

Chancing to look up, Bill saw that they had company. A ten-foot leopard seal was attempting to bite the strobe.

The animal was irritated, he thinks, by the intermittent flash. He had never seen a leopard seal so close.

Of all seals, the leopard is the most snakelike in build and animus. It is a big seal, yet lithe and sinuous. This particular leopard gathered itself like a cobra and struck repeatedly at the strobe. Bill began squeezing the shutter. The face illuminated in each cold stroboscopic glare was a death's head. The thin, lipless mouth ran like an incision back behind the eyes. The incision was stitched at intervals by the lines of whiskers, like crosshatch teeth on a Halloween mask. Bill had seen that mouth often before, from a safe elevation on the ice, as the leopards cruised offshore of penguin rookeries. The jaws of most were smeared with penguin blood. The stain was so set by frequent killing that the sea could not wash it off.

Of all marine mammals, only the leopard seal and the killer whale habitually eat warm-blooded prey. The leopard is the only *seal* to do so. It lives principally on penguins, but occasionally it takes a crabeater seal. It has yet to take a warm-blooded scientist or photographer, but a precedent of sorts existed. The seal's large eyes regarded Bill. Bill's strobe reflected from the silver lining of the tapetum.

The animal began racing around, darting in and out of visibility. When it came close, Bill's shutter froze it in different attitudes. On that roll of film, the Antarctic is a jungle, and the leopard seal is all the animals loose in it. In one flash the seal circles, as lithe and spotted as its namesake. In the next it hangs perpendicular, head lowermost and cocked toward the camera—a heavy-bodied python dangling from an unseen branch. Through successive frames its shape changes continually, as fluid and protean as a creature in myth.

Bill looked down and saw that the scientist was gone. Bubbles rose, marking his flight along the transect line toward shore. This was a rapid departure from the buddy system, but Bill understood. He was frightened himself, though not so badly as the scientist. He does not share the belief of many antarctic workers that leopard seals are extremely dangerous. The close fly-bys that others interpret as threats, Bill interprets as curiosity.

He kicked up slowly toward the surface, and the seal followed. When they were thirty feet from the top, Bill looked down. The seal was looking up at him. As Bill watched, the seal glanced down at the bubbles rising from the retreating scientist. The seal was interested. It took a last look up at Bill. Then it dove toward the bubbles.

When Bill again met the scientist, both of them safe on land, he learned that the leopard had chased circles around the man all the way to shore.

At home in Maine, on leaving the house at night, Bill switches on a bulb beneath the leopard seal's portrait. The seal, lit spookily from below, is supposed to scare burglars as badly in reproduction as it scared the scientist in life.

There are other Curtsinger photographs on the walls. Two of them, hung side by side, show penguins on antarctic pan ice. Bill shot them seconds apart, from the vantage of a low cliff. The prints are in black and white—on penguins in Antarctica color film is wasted. The penguins are Adelies, ninety-six of them. In the first photograph, ninety-six starched shirts face the camera. In the second, ninety-six black tails scatter from it, spiky wings upraised in terror. The ice looks like a ballroom after a bomb scare. It is not the presence of the photographer that has caused the disruption, nor any noise made by the camera. Between the two exposures, a leopard seal has hauled out on the ice.

What interests Bill most about this photograph of frightened penguins is less the penguins than the intervals between. The birds are spaced evenly, he points out. There are no panicked clumps of them. Each maintains its territory, even now, confronted by its mortal enemy. The Adelies scatter in perfect order, each bird buffered by the elbow room its individuality requires. Bill has seen these invisible circles around all the animals he's photographed everywhere—around wolves, around crows, around beaver—but they are especially apparent beneath the sea. Underwater the geometry becomes three-dimensional. The wolf's circle on the tundra becomes for whale or seal a sphere. The sphere surrounding the spotted dolphins of Hawaii is tight. Spotted dolphins will swim right up to you. The sphere around Hawaii's spinner dolphins, a smaller cousin that hunts farther inshore, is larger. Spinners are shy and won't come so close. The spheres of the fin whale and the blue whale are so voluminous that no underwater photographer has ever managed to enter and record one of the great animals swimming along at the center. The sphere of the gray whale is enterable, but not for long. "I've seen gray whales actually jump," Bill says. "They're startled by you. It's happened with every one I've ever seen. They don't have their feet connected with the earth, so the whole body jerks. And then they swim away like hell."

The dimensions of the sphere change with circumstances. In Newfoundland once, a trapped humpback whale, its flukes tangled in a cod net, allowed Bill to approach to within three meters of its rostrum, then began bobbing its head in warning. Bill visited on successive days, and the head-bobbing began always when he crossed that line. Three meters was the magic distance for this whale. In happier times its sphere surely had been larger,

Leopard seal, Anvers Island, Antarctic Peninsula

but in this situation the whale was content with three meters. With capelin, the schooling fish that Newfoundland humpbacks eat, the territorial circles become visible, as if treated with dye. Diving to photograph capelin, Bill has seen the school retreat from him in an arc so perfect it might have been inscribed by compass. Life in the ocean is built of this geometry of emptiness. Curtsinger's life is dedicated to entering the spheres, to crossing the magic lines.

The negative space of the penguin picture fascinates the photographer in Curtsinger, or the amateur naturalist in him, or the something else entirely. Occasionally he stops before the penguins and stares.

Not all the loft's photographs are of animals. Two color prints of an old cape lighthouse hang on the wall above the spotting scope. The first photo Bill shot from a distance. It shows the whitewashed keeper's house in the foreground, and behind it the whitewashed, thick-walled, tapering brick tower of the light itself. The second is a close-up of the tower's doorway, a study in textures, with Kate seated nude against the bare brick, her knees drawn up under her chin. This lighthouse stands abandoned on a barren rock to the north. Available for ninety thousand dollars, it is Bill's wildest dream.

Bill Curtsinger is a conceptual settler, an imaginary homebuilder in the manner of Henry Thoreau. I have heard him tell Kate to ready herself soon for a move to Puget Sound, to San Diego, to San Francisco. Once, on the Kona Coast of Hawaii, seated beside him on the floor of a renovated coffee shack, I saw the photographer look

covetously around him. We were on the floor because there were no chairs. The wallpaper was of hundred-pound burlap sacks stamped "Kona Coffee." The roof was corrugated tin. It was set on rollers, because in the old days, in sunny weather, the coffee workers rolled it back to dry the beans. The light inside was dim and stained by chlorophyll, for outside dark-green coffee trees impinged on all sides. Bill looked from the tin roof to Kate. He advised her to get ready for the move to a coffee shack in Kona.

It is not necessary, though, that the sites for his imaginary settling be distant or exotic. Each time Bill drives past Crowley's Lobster Pound, an unused building at the foot of Yates Street in his own hometown, he peers through the unwashed windows at the neglected tanks inside. He imagines what a fine one-man marine-science station the old place would make.

But all these plans are more or less playful. About the lighthouse, Bill is serious. He would sell his house at Biddeford Pool instantly and buy the lighthouse, he claims, if it were up to him.

"But what could you do with a lighthouse, really?" I ask.

He rolls his eyes. "What couldn't you do with it?" he asks back. Then he amplifies, describing some of the things a marine photographer and his artist wife might do with a lighthouse. When he is through, he looks dreamily out the window.

"Why don't you do it, then?"

For a moment he continues to gaze out the window, then his head swings slowly toward the kitchen. "Kate?"

Adelie penguins, moments before a leopard seal has hauled out on the ice

he asks, hopelessly, pathetically. Kate refuses to answer. She continues washing dishes. Her silence makes him bold —perhaps he can carve a small beach-head in the Normandy of her lighthouse position. "Come on, Kate." Not so pathetic this time.

"Billy, I'm not moving to a lighthouse. What about all our friends here? We still have to pay for *this* house."

The island is wonderful, Kate says, but not to live on. It wouldn't be sensible to live isolated on a rock. Billy, whose invisible circle in the world has a radius consider-

ably greater than his wife's, gives up—for the time being. He looks dreamily outside again.

Below his window, a narrow path runs seaward through the poplars. It comes to a plank bridging a marshy depression, then resumes on the far side, curving off through fallen leaves. At the path's midpoint, hanging from a tree like a buck strung up to cool, is a dead television tube. Bill threw the television out the loft window one night and later hung its tube in triumph on the tree. Twenty yards

Adelie penguins, the moment after

past the corpse of the television, the path ends at the door of the cottage Bill uses as his office.

This small cottage in Maine is a monument to that gray reef shark in West Fayu Atoll. The summer after the shark attacked him, Bill was laid up, occupied with machine therapy and the daily soaking of his hand. In the course of that summer, he and a friend built the cottage. Bill worked almost entirely right-handed. He was able to hold nails in his left, but otherwise it was little use to him. It's a snug cottage all the same. On the ground floor is a kitchenette,

a bathroom, and the office. A ladder leads upstairs to a bedroom turret. The turret is small, but has big windows and a view of dunes and ocean.

In the cottage, as in the loft, marine mammals dominate the decor. On the bedroom pillowcase, an embroidered male killer whale cavorts with an embroidered female. On the kitchenette's paper napkins, cartoon whales spout. In the office, against pine walls, hang several reproductions of drawings by Larry Foster. One shows two scuba divers swimming with cameras alongside the eye of a blue whale.

This is an exercise of Foster's imagination. No diver has ever been so fortunate. Bill dreams, though, of finding himself someday in this spot. The blue whale is the largest creature ever to exist on this planet, and in Foster's drawing the two divers are insignificant beside it, like fleas on the head of a forbearing, gentle-eyed hound. A second drawing shows two flensers, their long-handled knives in hand, working on the carcass of another blue whale. The two men look like lonely janitors cleaning up a gymnasium. The third Foster drawing is a color chart showing various whales in their relative sizes. This one was signed in place by the artist himself, and the signature runs off the paper onto the pine of the wall. "He's the Audubon of Cetacea," Bill says of Larry Foster. "He's the first guy to paint these things as if they weren't Goodyear blimps."

Foster's ability to convey the grace of living whales is due in part, thinks Bill, to his skill as an artist, but also to the meticulousness of his research. Bill and other marine photographers send him their reject pictures, and these Foster ponders. Photographs too dim, or too bright, or too out of focus to succeed as photographs, yet which give some hint at how a whale raises its rostrum to breathe, or dips a great pectoral fin to turn; some suggestion as to a whale's true dimensions in life—dimensions different from those in death, when, slack and unbuoyed by ocean, the whale lies on a factory ship or beach—these are the foundation for Foster's whales.

"He's unlike any other person I've ever met," Kate testifies. "Larry doesn't even get his feet wet. We've tried to get him to go see whales. In Hawaii it's *guaranteed* you'll see them. But he doesn't want to go—that's time away from his studio."

This dry-footed interest in whales is very different from Bill Curtsinger's interest. Bill is often uneasy with whale rapture at a remove. But in Foster he senses a true fellow spirit and he is glad to send Larry photographs.

"Does he send them back?" I ask.

Bill rolls his eyes. "From time to time I ask him for an inventory."

Against one office wall stands a small picture editor. The editor has a small, roll-out light table for viewing slides in bunches, and a ten-inch internal-projection screen for studying them enlarged. Above the editor, taped to the side of a bookcase, is a breathless letter from Hubert Pepper, another artist to whom Curtsinger sends pictures. The letterhead reads, "Hubert Pepper, Wildlife Artist, Royal Forest of Dean, Gloucestershire," and the letter says:

"My Dear Bill,

"I only posted a note to you yesterday. And now, twenty minutes after post today, after shelving the work I should be doing, I am *racing* to write you again. Oh! how I wish you were only a short journey away and that I could be painting on your doorstep instead.

"Bill. The fabulous poster arrived today. I remember saying rather tartly to you that Larry Foster only painted (or drew) his works from photographs. Then, I had only seen the Humpback breaching after the Balcombe photo. But, now. I take it all back and grovel. The work is beautiful and I only wish it had been I that guided the brush.

"It is a delightful poster. The next step is to bring closer the details of the lovely creatures and extend the range of the work to the extent that light and movement will allow. HERE is your mission! Please do not overlook me. Send me the best you can spare of the pictures you have.

"Bill—again I wish I was able to *Shout* to emphasize my feelings. Bill, you have the underwater seals. They are so different to the animals we have learned to treasure ashore. They are full of light, sinuous grace. Have you any *vitulina* or any other species underwater?

"I cannot repay. I can merely slave and rush before I'm popped into a box to get it down on paper or canvas and let others know.

"Yours, Hubert"

Beneath Hubert's signature is the blue wash of a watercolor sketch, which the artist has appended as a sort of wordless postscript. The sketch shows a monk seal, and Pepper has captured a good deal of the light, sinuous grace of the animal. He has repaid Bill after all.

Curtsinger, Hubert Pepper, Larry Foster, and other whale interpreters of the world keep in touch, exchanging materials and helping one another out. There is some of the same interchange between Bill and various sea-mammal scientists. The correspondence with scientists is perhaps slightly less cordial. It is Bill's impression that jealousies run deeper in the sciences than in the arts. But monographs by Edward Mitchell and Paul Dayton, zoologists he respects, lie on the cluttered desk, several of them prefaced with handscrawled notes from the author. On top of the pile is a glossy print of a pup harp seal nursing, and to it Bill has clipped an address, "Henry James, Dept of Psychology, Dalhousie University, Halifax, Nova Scotia." Long ago Dr. James asked if Bill had ever noticed a mother harp seal nursing with both nipples everted, a question Bill remembered recently, when, in reviewing his prints, he looked closely at this one. In it, the elongated white furball of the baby seal noses its dark and mottled mother, both of whose nipples are indisputably, beyond all academic cavil, everted. Photographic evidence for Dr. James.

A portrait of Robinson Jeffers hangs beside the door.

Jeffers is not a marine mammal, precisely, but no poet has written better about the meeting of sea and land, and he is Bill's favorite. There is a photo, too, of Bill and Bora Merdsoy sitting in red Unisuits at the edge of an ice lead. They are not marine mammals, either, but they are about to do a convincing imitation. In a moment they will slide in the water, following harp seals under the ice. The dark lead is full of slush ice, and their legs dangle casually in. Their faces are sober as they check over their equipment.

The bookshelf is occupied almost entirely by sea books. There are books on cetaceans, fish, and scuba-diving. There are a number of books on Antarctica. There is *Year of the Seal,* and *Moby Dick,* and a green-backed row of issues from the *Journal of Mammalogy,* collected by Bill for their articles on marine mammals.

There is "The Uniqueness of Carbon," a textbook chapter xeroxed for Bill by Bora. Bora sent the chapter in desperation. When he and Bill are alone together at sea, waiting for a whale to surface again, or when they're ashore, waiting out bad weather, Bill plagues him with questions about biology. Bora can't escape the questions—the Zodiac is only twelve feet long—so he has undertaken to shut Bill up by schooling him.

On the shelf also, as a kind of curiosity, is a prospectus from an outfit called Dolphin Embassy. The prospectus is slick and expensive. Its cover shows the Dolphin Embassy logo, in which a stylized man and dolphin are hooked together like trapeze artists, pivoting at the loins, if a dolphin can be said to have loins. The suggestion is sexual. The dolphin appears to be smiling.

"The Dolphin Embassy," begins the prospectus, "is a floating interspecies communication station dedicated to long term human-dolphin interaction in the open sea. During this joint American-Australian venture, scientists and artists will collaborate on experiments designed to create a deeper interspecies awareness.

". . . Early instruments were bulky and the analytical methods used during this time displayed a crude insensitivity toward the human/dolphin interface. Unfortunately our culture has underestimated the intelligence of dolphins and whales and has made serious diplomatic errors in our ethical and moral obligations toward the species."

An artist's impression of the Embassy shows a space-age vessel shaped like a pumpkin seed. The drawing has the tone of those hopeful, city-of-the-future illustrations that appeared in Sunday supplements in the nineteen fifties. A dolphin leaps, obligingly, to be photographed by a diver lounging on the stern. Another dolphin has entered a hatch and swum to a pool within the ship, where several humans are smiling down on it. In the ocean around the boat, humans and dolphins frolic together; one big, happy, interspecific family.

This is only the beginning, Dolphin Embassy promises. In the 1990s a second, larger embassy will follow, if all goes according to plan. In this embassy, two forward nodes will be "interspecies living rooms," and the bridge will have dual dolphin-human controls. There will be a "Brain Room," where the two species will communicate with light and sound pens.

The prospectus introduces the first generation of "ambassadors." They are men in their early thirties, for the most part, with backgrounds in industrial design, architecture, and media communication. They bring a clean-slate approach to cetology. Their single common qualification is that none has any experience with dolphins or whales. One ambassador, Curtis Schreier, whom the prospectus describes as a man of "high technical skill and benevolent character," is quoted within:

False killer whales, Hawaii

"As I worked on the design, I realized that it has some really fiction-sounding implications. When dolphins have their first chance to observe a land-based tool-using culture, will they decide that life in the sea is too limited? What will their desires and aspirations be then?"

A report from Australia, where the boat is to be built, brings the project up to date: "Communication experiments aboard the Dolphin Embassy are being designed to contact the alien aqua-terrestrial intelligence of the cetacean. Music, meditation, sensory isolation, deep underwater swimming and dream yoga will be among the tools used to transcend behavioral conditioning of land based industrial society. With the correct mental attitude, communication will evolve naturally out of love, trust, and friendship."

The ambassador from the order Primates will keep pace with the ambassadors from the order Cetacea by means of the "Dol-Fin Swimming System," according to the prospectus. The system will employ a suit of synthetic dolphin skin, specially treated to make its surface porpoise-shiny. The ambassador's feet fit side by side into two openings in a dolphinlike set of flukes. His hands fit into circular hand flippers. He breathes through a blowhole behind the neck portion of his wrap-around helmet. "It is hoped," says the prospectus, "that through practice and familiarity in general, man will be able to achieve at least fifty percent efficiency, in relation to body weight and size, of the comparable cetacean."

A drawing shows a human ambassador in a Dol-Fin suit. The ambassador looks uncannily like the Creature from the Black Lagoon. He holds his circular hand flippers stiffly at his sides. His pose is puzzled, as if the Creature, on emerging from its black lagoon, had been abruptly asked to play ping-pong, and with *two* paddles. His feet are encased in their dolphin flukes. His expression is resigned. He looks like a gangster on his way to bottom of the East River in cement shoes.

Bill Curtsinger, tapping the drawing, shakes his head. "You'd never in a million years get me in a suit like that. It's sure suicide. Humans just don't have the musculature to work something like that.

"This whole interspecies trip . . . I spend most of my life trying to get close to these animals. I'd love for it to be true. But I've never seen a single microscrap of evidence to make me believe it. I'd *love* to believe it. It would make everything I do *more* important.

"It sure would make my life easier. If dolphins were into meeting with me, if they wanted to meditate with me and have a psychic connection with me, it sure would be a lot easier to get close to them and do my job. But we

Dusky dolphins, Patagonia

flatter ourselves. They're just not that interested in people.

"This mystical whale cult bothers me because it doesn't have anything to do with whales.

"The thing with dolphins is, they're so unbelievably *adapted,* in every little bend and curve of their bodies. So much more so than any other animal I've ever seen, in any environment. I guess I notice it because I'm in there so much, and yet I'm so out of place, compared to them. I'm better in the water than most people, but I'm so remote from dolphins, from what dolphins can do. Watching a dolphin swim is like watching a cheetah run."

"What about their intelligence?" I ask. "Don't you think they're intelligent?"

" 'Intelligent.' Everybody uses the word intelligence loosely, I think. It's used by people through their experience with Flipper, and Sea World, and all those places where the animal is really dependent on humans. Where it performs imbecile acts for food reward. Everybody thinks they're so intelligent because they do these tricks for man.

"They're adapted. They're wicked adapted to their environment. That's a better word to use. Why do they have to be smart, anyway? People always have to attach a word like that to a foreign thing like a dolphin. Those animals constantly blow my mind — *they just blow my mind* — but I don't have to think about how bright they are."

"What is it, then, that attracts you to dolphins."

"It's . . . their intelligence." He laughs at himself. "I don't know, it's confusing to me. It's their awareness. That's a much better word. I'm comfortable with that."

"Their awareness about you?"

"Their awareness about me? Yes, about me. If I compare them to fish. Fish don't choose to spend time in the water near a diver. A marine mammal sometimes chooses to spend time in the water with you. *That's* pretty interesting. 'Curiosity' is another word I'm comfortable with. Marine mammals express themselves in a curious way a great deal."

On the bookshelf, amidst all the thousands of words on sea mammals, all the sea-mammal photos and representations, sit two small samples of the real item. One is a tin of Nanyo Boeki Kaisha Brand Barbecued Whale Meat, containing six ounces of "Whale-meat, chilly, garlic, soy-sauce, sesame-seeds, sugar and spices." The other tin holds seven ounces of Arctic Brand Newfoundland Seal.

When I ask Bill about the tins, he picks the tin of harp seal off the shelf and contemplates it.

"I found the whale meat, of all places, on a shelf in Satawal, in Micronesia. I got the seal meat off a shelf in Newfoundland. It's a strange thing. A little plug of an animal like that. I don't know — I don't know why I got it. I've been with these animals, and they're so important to me. And that's all somebody's experience of a harp seal — in that can. When I pushed the grocery cart past the shelf and saw it, my mind filled with all sorts of thoughts. I had to have it. I wanted to think about it some more, that plug of an animal."

He sets the tin of harp seal, his Yorick's skull, back in its place.

9. Pagophile

IN THE GULF of St. Lawrence, the first time he followed harp seals under the ice, Bill worked alone. "It was the most insane thing I've ever done," he admits. "They had a diving partner for me, but he'd never been in cold water and he'd never worn a Unisuit. We went in a lead, down about thirty feet, and the first thing he did was drop his weight belt. I saw him rocketing toward the surface. A weight belt is so important with a Unisuit, which has all that buoyancy. He slammed his head on the underside of the ice. I escorted him to the lead, and he never came in again."

The Unisuit is a dry suit, insulated by air instead of water. It is a Swedish invention and costs about $400. Bill started wearing Unisuits in 1972. In recent years the suits have been catching on, and today most professional divers working in cold waters use them. From a valve on the Unisuit, a hose runs under the diver's arm and into the low-pressure valve on his regulator. On the right breast is a button to inflate the suit. On the left is a purge button to deflate it. A middleweight like Bill Curtsinger, on pushing his right button, swells into a Haystack Calhoun. The suit is difficult to get into. The diver needs help, for the zipper starts at the top of his back. He needs assistance as far down as his crotch; from there he's on his own. The neck seal must be tight, and the diver must be sure its neoprene lies flat against his skin. The outfit is heavy and feels strange. In a normal wetsuit, Bill wears eighteen to twenty pounds of lead on his belt. In a Unisuit he wears thirty-five.

"It's a professional piece of diving equipment," he says.

"You have to learn about it. You need to constantly think and make adjustments. If you're too buoyant, and you're holding your breath as you go up, you can get an embolism and kill yourself."

When his partner failed to handle his Unisuit, Bill was just as glad to have the man stay on top of the ice. "A lot of people say it's crazy diving alone. Oftentimes that's not true. If you have to worry about somebody all the time, first, you're not going to get any work done, and second, if he's somebody you have to *worry* about, what good is he going to be in an emergency?"

In this instance, though, diving alone *was* crazy. Bill grew increasingly uneasy under the ice. One day a male seal began behaving aggressively, making close, fast passes. Bill left the water and did not go back. "With a diver I trusted, I wouldn't have worried about it for a moment. But I was alone down there. If there's just one of you, animals act differently. Two of you is an entirely different thing. Sharks are a perfect example. Or going into bars. You're just safer with a friend. It was just too crazy down there. They weren't paying me enough."

When he returned the next year to photograph harp seals, in March 1975, this time working for *National Geographic*, Bill hired a new partner. The new man was Bora Merdsoy, who had previous experience with Unisuits in the cold waters of the Canadian Arctic. The two divers hit it off from the start.

"Before I met Billy, I thought he would be much older," Bora says. "You know, this *National Geographic*

Harp seal, Gulf of St. Lawrence

photographer. I was flabbergasted that we had a helicopter at our disposal. I thought it would be a boss-nigger relationship.

"My experience before, at Arctic-4, hadn't been so good. It was a very regimented set-up. We dove three times a week, four to six hours in the water sometimes. It was mundane work, going along from plant to plant. That's how I got used to Unisuits and learned how to tolerate cold water.

"*Tolerate.* Sometimes it's enjoyable to get really cold, crazy as that sounds. Go home and eat, and you're out like a light. You wake up the next morning and you want to do it all over again.

"When I met Billy, we were wearing almost identical clothes. I was even a little older than he was. I took him out to my place—it was a shack—and he loved it. It was like I had found my long-lost brother.

"Three days after I met the guy, he wants to get out on the ice before dawn. It was a cold miserable f—ing day. I hadn't had my coffee. I just wanted to go back and sit in the helicopter. He wanted this one picture, a dawn shot.

"Billy's taught me an awful lot. It's difficult to put into words. He's taught me stuff about mechanics, and stuff about cameras, but also how to look at things. He taught me about forgetting your little physical needs. Perseverence—I just don't have the perseverence he has. That's what sometimes pisses him off about me. If something's happening, he'll stay the limit, until something gives out —air or film. When things are cooking, he has boundless energy. Energy to get the picture or see the novel thing.

That's why he sees the things he does. I think that's why he's impatient with scientists sometimes.

"He wanted his dawn picture, and he got it. I hadn't realized that, about a professional photographer—he has in his mind the picture he wants. There must be a million pictures of harp seals on ice, but I've never seen another like that one."

If there were, indeed, a million pictures of harp seals on ice, there were very few of harp seals *under* it. That was Bill's specialty, and that, mainly, was what he was after. They scouted for seals in the helicopter. It cost $250 an hour, so they had to find seals quickly. They wore their Unisuits and all their diving gear. They used double tanks, and their belts alone, in compensating for all that buoyancy, weighed eighty pounds apiece. They flew into battle ponderously, like knights, the pilot doubling as their tender, or squire. All three men scanned the ice for what they needed; a promising concentration of breathing holes and a spot to land safely without disturbing the seals. From the air, as they hovered, the seal colony was laid out like a lesson. They saw the dark, pointed sacks of adult harp seals hauled out beside the leads; the white, hard-to-see pups beside their mothers; the breathing holes, asterisked by tracks the seals had made in crawling in and out; the spattered orange trails of afterbirth. It was the pilot who decided on the spot. Finding a place he liked, he dropped the copter down.

The harp seal, *Pagophilus groenlandicus,* "the ice-lover of Greenland," wanders in summer over much of the Arctic.

Harp seal pup

It ranges north of Svalbard, Franz Josef Land, and Novaya Zemlya to within 500 miles of the pole. It hunts the waters around all of Greenland except the northern tip. It roams westward past Baffin Island and into Hudson's Bay, eastward past Severnaya Zemlya to the Taymyr Peninsula in the Soviet Union. In October and November, when the northern seas begin to freeze, the seals turn south. The pack ice marches after them, and the seals retreat before it, hundreds of thousands of them. In February and March, when the sea ice to the south is thickest—safest for rearing pups—the females haul out. They give birth on the frozen ocean off the Magdalen Islands in the Gulf of St. Lawrence, off Labrador, off eastern Greenland, and in the White Sea off the U.S.S.R.

Few creatures see first light on a harsher landscape, or draw first breath in more bitter air. The harp-seal pup must be, and is, a miracle of cold-weather design. Its pelt, at first glance pure white, has at second glance a fuzzy immateriality. The hairs are translucent. The sun shines through to warm the skin, and the pelt holds the heat close —a "greenhouse effect." The pup begins life at fifteen pounds—not much bulk for a warm-blooded creature that will spend its life in cold seas—but the transfer of substance from the mother is so speedy and efficient that in three weeks the pup weighs one hundred pounds. This neat trick is all the neater in that *P. groenlandicus* is not a large seal. Females weigh less than four hundred pounds; in less than a month they give more than a quarter of themselves. The magic is in the milk, forty-five percent fat, ten percent protein.

The pup's eye is a high artifact of accommodation. It has a light-gathering lens nearly as round as the whale's, and its retina, like the whale's, is backed by a light-amplifying tapetum, for like the whale the pup will do most of its adult hunting in the dimness underwater. Yet unlike the whale's eye, the pup's first opens on a white, glassy, dazzling world. The seal eye sees well both in darkness and in light, in water and in air. In the glare on the ice, the pup's pupils narrow to vertical slits. Underwater, when the pup on its first clumsy swim looks down into the dark, strong dilator muscles open the pupils wide. A pronounced corneal astigmatism aids vision in the water. When the pup returns to the air, the pupil narrows again to a slit, which lies parallel to the astigmatic axis, thereby eliminating the astigmatism. The eyes of baby harp seals, huge, dark, lustrous, look out innocently from a thousand advertisements protesting their slaughter. They break hearts in warm, well-lighted living rooms all over the world. But those eyes are full of something better than appeal; they are full of function.

Canada permits its sealing fleet, the fleet of Norway, and Canada's coastal inhabitants to take 180,000 harp seals annually from Canadian whelping grounds. The harp-seal population of the Western Atlantic, from which these 180,000 are subtracted, is less than a million. The present level of harvest is clearly not sustainable. The harp seal is in decline. Most of the seals killed are pups. The white pelt so indispensable to *P. groenlandicus* in infancy may well do the species in. When, three-weeks old, the pup ceases its heroic bouts of nursing and begins to shed its whiteness for a grayer color, it does so not a moment too soon.

The helicopter landed, and Bill and Bora waddled like sumo wrestlers to the edge of the lead. The water in the lead was black, and slush ice floated there. The seals, when not using their breathing holes, rise for air at the leads, and the males tend to congregate there. Pausing at the edge, Bill or Bora screwed a regulator onto an extra air tank, attached the tank to a downline, and lowered it through the slush ice. The spare tank would hang at fifty or sixty feet, in case of emergency. Then the men followed themselves, entering the water with Unisuits slightly over-inflated. Bobbing on the surface, each rolled so that his purge button was highest, pressed it, and sank. Under-water, each man could feel and hear the stream of bubbles escaping from the circle of vents around the button. If he was sinking too fast, he would hit the other button to dump some air back in.

The first day, Bora wore a rope, though Bill told him it would not be necessary.

"I didn't know if there would be currents," Bora says, "or what the visibility would be. But Billy was right—there were no currents, and you could always see the hole you came through. My job was to keep the hole in sight. Usually that meant I was above him, but sometimes it meant I was deeper. I'd bang on my tank if he strayed too far away, or I'd wave him back. We hung that yellow tank under the hole, too, to make it more obvious."

When Bill first entered the water, his face felt cold for five or ten seconds, then he no longer noticed. His body was warm. His first Unisuit had leaked, but this one was fine. Diving this way was warmer than skiing.

He swam down into an inverted landscape. Upside-down hills of ice rolled away on all sides of him. The floes, crunched together by wind and tide, had "raftered," push-ing up or down as pressure ridges above and below the surface. Above the surface, the buckled slabs were blocky and sometimes snow-covered. Below, the ocean had sculpt-ed the ice into fluid curves. The submarine walls were very like those carved by Southwestern rivers in Navajo

Sandstone, except that the scale here was smaller and the warm colors of the desert were replaced by cold blue-greens. The harp-seal canyons did not plummet sheerly down to a silty Colorado; they plummeted up to the lead, a bright antiriver of sky and sunlight. Blocks of ice floated in the lead—the clouds in that sky—and seals were the birds. In places along the canyon walls was a submarine talus of ice slabs. Everywhere were caves and caverns. The harp seals went spelunking, entering and exiting the caves freely. They sat on the massive marble chairs and tables of sunken slabs, anchoring themselves with the claws on their flippers, watching the progress of the orange Unisuits.

The Unisuits swam down into an underworld of sound. The chatter of the colony buffeted them, a music anything but harplike. Harp seals are named for the dark, lyre-shaped markings on their backs, not for their voices. "The noise!" remembers Bill. "Geez, it was like a barnyard." The seals sounded like hybrid armies of pig-birds gather-ing at troughs, or like nursing puppies, or like hordes of clowns honking the bulbs on their noses.

The water was clear except for some ctenophores. Bill and Bora saw no fish, except for one ray, and that came up in the mouth of a seal. The year before, Bill had glimpsed a pebbly bottom, but this time they saw nothing but darkness. The seals, they suspected, could usually reach bottom, though the ice was forever drifting, and the depth continually changed. Sometimes the ice drifted close in-shore of the Magdalen Islands, sometimes into deeper waters, so the bottom was always different underneath. The harp seals' floe, then, was like that flying island in *Gulliver's Travels,* except that the residents had no control. Falling asleep over one stretch of bottom, they would wake, shuffle to the lead, and dive to find themselves over a new stretch. If harp seals have a cosmology, the ice is the universal center, and the sea floor orbits.

Underwater Bora studied his new employer. He was im-pressed. "Billy's an excellent diver," he says today. "He's very smooth. Being underwater is second nature to him. With most people you have to watch so they don't hurt themselves. With Billy, that's not even a question."

March was mating time, and Bill and Bora swam into the middle of that ritual. They watched double-helical courtship dances, suitors spurned, happy endings. They became participants themselves. One day a young harp seal kissed Bill's mask.

"He has an attraction for animals, anyway," says Bora. "Dogs will bark at me, but they come right up to him. Billy's childlike, without being childish. That's one of his attractions to people, as well as animals."

For the kissing episode, Bill has an explanation. "Often

immature or naive males will come around. I don't think they understand the mating game, you know? With a lot of animal species, juveniles will follow the breeding population, not knowing quite what to do. You see gangs of them going around. Adelie penguins are like that. Young harp seals are real curious. They almost always come up to you. If you were more like a seal, they'd hang around more. I stroked the underside of one seal who was hanging around, and it pushed its face into my mask.

"You pick up sexual innuendos. No scientist would buy that information, I guess, but if you're human, you sort of know all of them—all those cues. I don't have any desire to make love to a seal. It's just that . . . it's just that every once in a while you pick up one of these sexual cues, just like you would with your own kind.

"Underwater, most animals are really curious about your face mask and the camera dome. That's always what they seem to cue in on. They know where your eyes are in the mask, and I guess the glass dome looks like a big eye to them. When a whale looks at you, as he goes by, he's not looking at your toes. He's looking at your eyes or your camera dome. Sea lions, too. The harp seal that pushed its face against my mask was especially curious—more curious than the others.''

The Unisuit was not perfect protection against the chill. Whichever part of Bill's body was lowermost soon felt it. When his legs got cold, he turned upside down in the water and the air in the Unisuit rose to warm them. When his torso and arms got cold, he reverted. He could work equally well in either position. In the sea, up and down are directions important to mammals only when it's time to go up and breathe.

Bill had installed oversized control knobs on his Ocean-eye, because in cold waters his hands get too cold to turn normal-sized knobs. In the Gulf of St. Lawrence, his hands sometimes got too cold anyway, despite the big knobs and the Unisuit gloves. The gloves had three fingers. (Five-fingered gloves with sufficient insulation would be too thick to be workable, so three of the diver's fingers must share, while thumb and forefinger are on their own.) When Bill's hands got too numb to function, he would hold the camera between his knees and raise his arms above his head. The ascending air ballooned the gloves. From the now-spacious neoprene fingers, he withdrew his own. He balled his fist in the glove's palm and worked his fingers. After a minute, they were warm enough to return to their places and resume their tasks, adjusting F-stop and exposure.

For the harp seals, of course, no such odd postures were necessary. The seals did without gloves, low-pressure valves, inflated suits, spare tanks, and face masks, and they seemed to be perfectly comfortable. The Scandinavian design in the Unisuits was good; the pinniped design was better.

The seal's pelt was its first, scanty line of defense against the cold. In phocid seals like the harp seal, the hair is not so effective a barrier to heat loss as in otarid seals like the fur seal, but it helps a little. (The phocids are the crawling seals, descended from otterlike land carnivores. They have no external ears, and their power is in their hind flippers. The otarids are the walking seals, descended from a bear-like land carnivore. They have small external ears and their power is in their shoulders and front flippers.) In both seal families, the hair grows in bundles. In each bundle a single flattened guard hair protects a cluster of underhairs. The underhairs trap air bubbles, which serve as insulation. In fur seals, each cluster has as many as seventy underhairs, trapping so much air that the skin beneath never gets wet. In the phocids, there are only two to five underhairs in each bundle. The harp seals and the rest of their phocid cousins, then, must rely more on the thermal layers underneath the pelt.

When a phocid seal enters the water, a vascular constriction cuts off blood flowing to the skin and blubber. Skin temperature drops until it is only about one degree above that of the water, just warm enough that the skin does not freeze. The temperature gradient between skin and water is so slight that little heat is lost across it. Within its two-inch blanket of blubber, the harp seal stays toasty. The advantage of the phocid method over otarid is that thermal regulation is easier and more precise. Where an otarid like the fur seal must wave its hind flippers in the air to cool off, just as a husky pants and lolls its tongue, a phocid like the harp seal simply relaxes the arterioles in its skin, which fills with blood and releases body heat. The phocid plan is the more successful. Whether because of advantages in thermal regulation, or in its rear-flipper drive, or in something else, there are more than twice as many phocid models, and they range more widely, through more diverse habitats. The most cosmopolitan seal of all, the harbor seal, is a phocid.

The harp seal's unisuit of blubber, besides warming the seal, streamlines it, encloses it as a pressure vessel on deep dives, and serves as a fuel reserve in those lean times when the seal eats little, as in the breeding season. The seal's unisuit, unlike the neoprene kind, is malleable, molding itself to the flow of water. Ripples form in the seal's skin and blubber, eliminating turbulence and maintaining laminar flow.

Harp-seal country: leads, breathing holes, adults sleeping, pups nursing, stains of afterbirth

Harp-seal pups, dawn, Gulf of St. Lawrence

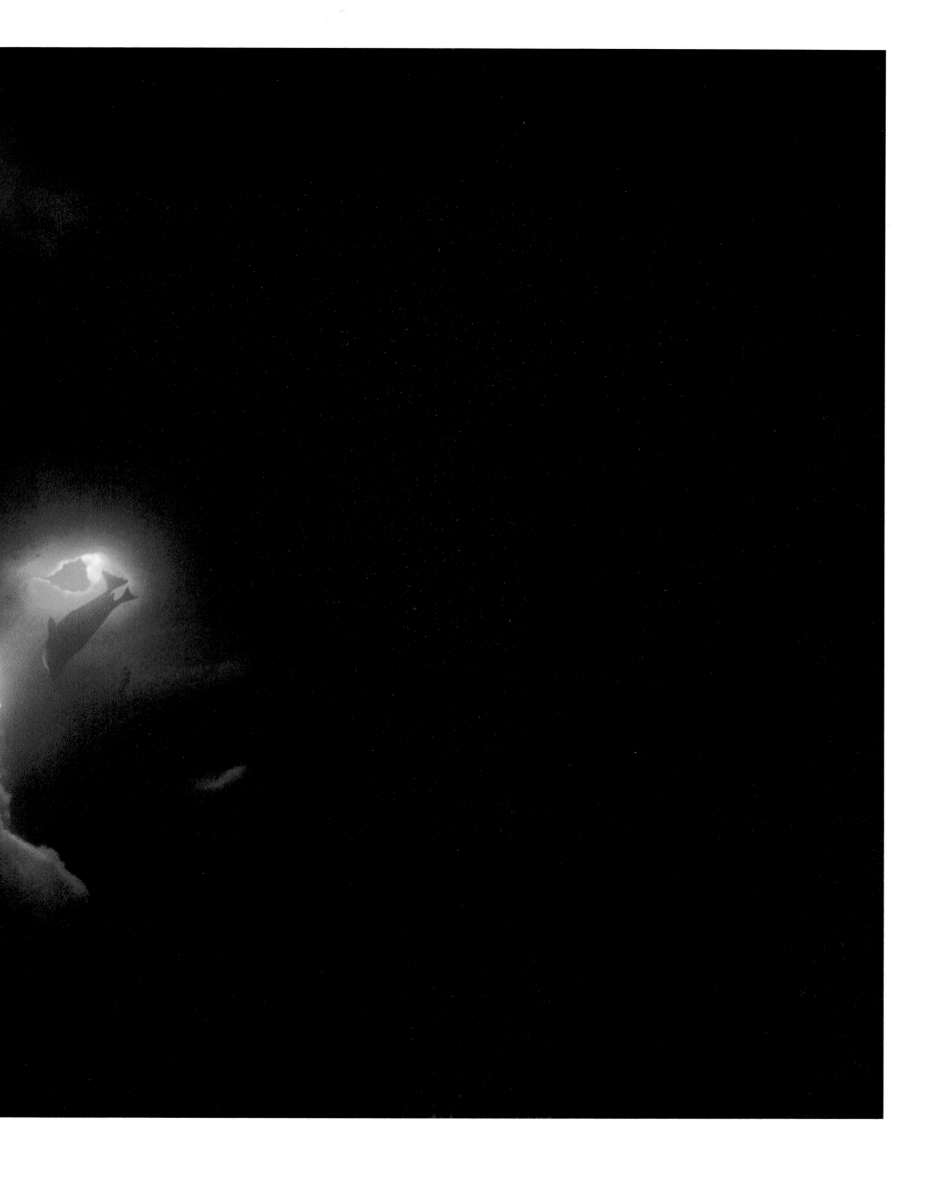

They all appear every now at the surface together, springing up so as to raise their heads and necks, and often their whole bodies out of the water. Their progress is pretty rapid; their actions appear frisky; and their general conduct is productive of amusement to the spectator. The sailors, when they observe such a shoal, call it a "Seal's Wedding."
—WILLIAM SCORESBY

Harp seal at breathing hole, Gulf of St. Lawrence

Harp seal and ice sculpture, Gulf of St. Lawrence

Hooded seal and pup, Gulf of St. Lawrence

The voice of the young seal when in pain or distress, is a whining cry, resembling that of a child. Seals appear to hear well when under water; music, or particularly a person whistling, draws them to the surface.

—WILLIAM SCORESBY

Harp seal and pup, Gulf of St. Lawrence

The animal within the suit has undergone modifications too, since its days on land as an otterlike animal. Its organs are those of a land mammal still, with a few extra wrinkles, like the hepatic sinus and caval sphincter of its circulatory system—but those land-mammal organs have developed special capabilities. A harp seal can dive below six hundred feet and stay under for thirty minutes. Diving, the seal does not draw a deep breath; it exhales, for inflated lungs would cause trouble at depth. The seal stores its oxygen in its blood, which is almost twice as plentiful, proportionately, as that of a human, and in the myoglobin of its muscles. Underwater, the seal enters the state called bradycardia. Its heart rate drops from around one hundred beats a minute to as few as four. Bradycardia occurs also in muskrats and beaver, in cetaceans, even in experienced human divers, but in seals it is most pronounced. Old seals, like old Indian fakirs, have learned to control their heart rates better than novices. In older seals, bradycardia begins sooner, slows the heart more, and lasts longer.

When the seal dives, oxygenated blood leaves its extremities and pools in the brain and vital organs. Much of the muscle activity is anaerobic, so the seal draws on its oxygen sparingly. The seal's nostrils in their relaxed state are closed. The moustachial pad presses against the nasal septum, sealing the nostrils, and the pressure of the dive only presses the pad tighter. As the depth increases, the lungs flatten, the seal's flexible ribs bend, and its whole being becomes more serpentine under the weight of the water. The pupils of the great eyes dilate to engulf the whole iris, and the seal hunts a dimness that to the human eye would look black.

The seal's tissues tolerate high carbon-dioxide levels. In a novice human diver, carbon dioxide trips an early warning system, sending a surge of panic through him, and he looks to the surface. Experienced divers learn to ignore the signal and stay down a little longer. For the harp seal, that warning is the faintest of tintinnabulations. It takes nearly forever to sound. When the bell does finally chime, twenty or thirty minutes after the seal has left the surface, down in the darkness six hundred feet beneath, the seal makes its way upward calmly but fast. The green glow above rapidly becomes brighter. The glow resolves itself into the undersea ice sculpture of the harp-seal's Emerald City. The seal picks the bright vein of a lead, or the sunny circle of a breathing hole, and it heads there. Its pupils narrow, its lungs uncrinkle and expand, its ribs unbend, its serpentine body becomes more seallike. It skims past the ice walls of the Emerald City, bobs above the floating slush-ice, and blows open its nostrils. It breathes.

At home in Biddeford Pool, Bill sometimes gives slide shows at the volunteer firehouse. He scratches joke captions and dialogue into the emulsion of slides he's taken of local types, and he mixes these in with serious photographs taken in the field. Among the latter are pictures of harp seals. The scenes under the ice cause a stir in the Biddeford Pool Volunteer Fire Department.

"The firemen ask me, 'How do you do that?'" Bill says. "It looks so crazy to them, under the ice. It looks like you might get trapped. They don't stop to think that the seals can always get out." Here Bill switches briefly to a Maine accent. "'Mightn't that close up on you, Bill?'" He switches back. "No, it doesn't close up."

It is kind of Bill to reassure the firemen, but what he tells them is not quite true. A hazard for all respiring life in cold seas is the freezing of breathing hole or ice lead. One of the purposes of the bowhead whale's limousine-sized pate is to break through the ice, and it can handle thicknesses of more than a foot. The walrus's dense skull is designed for a somewhat thinner exigency—ice up to eight inches thick. Bill and Bora lacked the heavy-duty craniums. In the Gulf of St. Lawrence, when the sun dropped low, temperatures plummeted, the slush ice in the leads began to freeze, and they had to be careful.

Once, swimming up toward the light after the day's last harp-seal picture, Bill rose as if to pass through the slush, and instead bumped into it. The slush was solid—the lead had frozen. Bora rose beneath. With the quick comprehension Bill values in his friend—without wasting time in testing the surface himself, Bora coolly began unharnessing his tanks for use as battering rams. He was just swinging them off when Bill, feeling his way along the translucent ceiling of their prison, found a weak spot he could poke through. Bora takes Bill's word for the part about his coolly removing his tanks. "I don't remember that. I was too scared."

Their internal alarms ceased clanging. For a moment, though, they had known the polar seal's pagophobia in finding itself locked out from life. Safe above the surface, spitting out their regulators, they knew the seal's gratitude, after the ice relents, for the sweetness of air.

Another time, Bora and Bill sat together at the edge of a lead, their legs dangling in the black water. As they checked over their gear before diving, they happened to look up. They saw the lead closing. The floe on the far side was advancing, and the lead, which a moment before had been twenty feet wide, now was fifteen. While they gazed, it closed to ten. Bora watched the pressure ridge buckling up. *It looks like a bulldozer is pushing it,* he remembers thinking. Then he swung his legs out of the water.

The ice was sometimes spooky, yet going under it, believes Bill, is the only way to find out about harp seals. As far as he can gather, he and Bora have spent more time underwater with harp seals than any scientist, and he finds this strange.

About scientists in general, Bill is often doubtful. He meets them often in the field, and often he is not impressed. "They forget that they're animals themselves," he says. "They forget about their instinctual sense. They're people—a lot of them are—who require all sorts of money to buy all sorts of gadgetry for things that could be accomplished in much simpler, better ways. Big-buck science. They remove themselves methodically from everything they're interested in.

"It's not like you have to *suffer* to get the data. But look, if you're interested in harp-seal behavior, it's crazy not to look around under the ice. None of these behaviorists do it. Ninety-nine percent of harp-seal activity takes place where scientists don't even get a look at it. They'll sit on top of the ice and say that harp seals don't feed in the mating season. If they just opened their minds up and poked their heads under, they'd see there was a lot of seal shit in the water. How did *that* get there, if the animals don't feed?"

Bill's thoughts on scientists transport him to the Arctic.

"In summer of 1977, I spent a month on an icebreaker in the Chukchi Sea, going after walruses. It makes me sick to think about it. Here was this 260-foot icebreaker, and a helicopter, and 250 humans, and 80,000 a day of the taxpayers' dollars, all for this total bungling. The primary mission of the research was to radio-tag a walrus. Which we never did. The only time they got a reading from a walrus was when me and this Coast Guard diving officer showed them how to do it.

"They needed my rubber boat to do their tagging. The first time the leader steps in, he puts a hole in Bloater. The tagging pole had sharp threads on the end, and he jammed it in where the floorboards meet the hull. All the times, all the places Bora and I have been in that rubber boat, we never put a hole in it.

"There were a dozen radio tags costing in excess of a thousand dollars apiece. The tag is fixed at the end of a long pole. A small explosive charge operates the hydrolics, which drives nails into the blubber and holds the tag there. That device represents what's wrong with a lot of science. We got a signal from the walrus for just as long as it took him to get to the nearest floe. They hadn't thought it one step further. They never thought about considering the underside of that ice. It has all these little grooves. It's even rougher than in the Gulf of St. Lawrence. It was very melted, sloppy, old, weak, mushy, convoluted, drifting sea ice. He made a beeline for the floe, went under and rubbed off the tag."

Remembering scientists, Bill's mind races south and west, at the speed of light, from the Chukchi Sea to the subtropics. He tells his best scientist horror story.

"In Hawaii once, off Maui, Chuck Nicklin and I were in the Zodiac following a whale, a single humpback. It was moving very slowly, about two hundred yards offshore. All of a sudden, I saw this shape following us. Chuck says, 'Shark.' It was a great big tiger shark. It was attracted by the motion of the white propeller, I think. I wanted to get out of there. I feel very vulnerable in that tiny rubber boat with a shark that size around.

"So we left. It took us five minutes to catch up with the whale. Then we spent ten minutes traveling with it. We assumed that fifteen minutes was enough to put the shark behind us. We never put two and two together.

"We got into the water in front of the humpback. The way we worked it, when both of us were in the water, one had to tow the boat. Chuck was in the better position, so I grabbed the bowline. I dragged the boat a while. It was murky, and not very interesting, so I climbed back in the boat. The whale moved off, and Chuck swam back to the boat. He had just hefted himself in and was lifting his flippers out when there was this swirl of motion behind him. It was the tiger shark. It had just missed him and was putting on the brakes. Chuck said, 'Hey!' and made a little joke, but it shook him up, and me too.

"That tiger shark was following the whale. It had some sort of interest in that solitary old humpback.

"So we left the area, and shortly afterward we ran into another group of humpbacks. They were jumping and flipping around. We followed them for three or four hours. We weren't chasing them—you can't get pictures that way. We were making big, wide berths, trying to get in front.

"We heard this honking, and this big, gray-green, ninety-foot tuna boat was coming right at us. We stopped. This person on the bridge was filming us, all the way up. He ran down from the bridge to the rail and started yelling us the Marine Mammal Act. He was a National Marine Fisheries biologist. He told us we were harassing whales, and that he had us on film.

"We were furious. We weren't harassing whales. We had been with the whales for four hours; if we were bothering them, they would have left. It's pretty much the whales' ballgame. If they want to go, they'll go. Humpbacks can dive for fifteen minutes, and when they come up, God knows where they'll be.

Harp seal and pup, Gulf of St. Lawrence

"The truth is, Chuck Nicklin almost bought the farm that day. And the reason he almost bought it was we were going overboard *not* to harass the whales—we were making such an effort to swim off from the boat.

"Later, when we came ashore that evening, I learned that this guy, this National Marine Fisheries biologist, had once had a permit to take more than three hundred gray whales. *He had killed more than three hundred whales.*"

Once, in the Gulf of St. Lawrence, diving under ice where science seldom ventured, Bill swam toward a breathing hole. Above, he knew, a female harp seal was lying on the ice. Beneath the hole, a male seal had stationed himself upright in the water. Seeing Bill, he vocalized and blew bubbles. The dollop of air wobbled up, like the talk balloon in a cartoon, but empty of words.

Bill thought he could read the missing language. It was something like "scram." He has never read in any monograph, or heard first-hand from any scientist, that bubble-blowing in marine mammals is a warning, but he's sure that is what it is. "I don't have anything to support it, but that's just what's happening. There's always a sound in association with the display. I just know that's what's happening."

From the green depths below the male seal, other dollops of bubbles were rising. It was as if a whole hierarchy of males was waiting in tiers beneath the female, working out, through threats and bubbles, their positions on the dominance ladder. It might have been interaction of an entirely different sort, of course. Bill didn't know. He couldn't see it. One of the things that draws him to the sea is the way it has of concealing so much more than it discloses.

The lower seals were not visible, but their sound filled the sea.

The coughs and barks of the seals on the ice were just the iceberg's tip of harp-seal noise. There was a separate world of sound beneath. Bill and Bora recorded it with hydrophones. In vocalizing under the ice, the seals enjoyed making a simple sound and repeating it once. Most common was a birdy *oink oink*. Two was their favorite number. The harp seal conversation had less variety than that of whales. It sounded more rudimentary. Whales have inhabited the sea for twice as long as seals, and they seem to have used the extra thirty million years well in building their vocabularies and refining their underwater elocution.

The individual harp seal's monologue was not particularly pretty music. But when you stopped listening to it, and began hearing instead the background it merged with —the collective babble of the species—the music was something else again. It was like ignoring the scrape of a single branch for the sound of the wind in the forest. The voices blurred with distance into a multitudinous whisper. The whisper suggested whole nations under the ice, and the vanished nations that preceded them. It might have been a song of pagophile history—the murmur of the thousands of generations that had wandered these icy seas at the top of the planet—and it was beautiful.

10. Newfoundland

THREE MONTHS AFTER leaving the harp seals in June 1975, Bill and Bora were in Newfoundland in pursuit of whales. Newfoundland looked the way Bill had always imagined Ireland: green meadows rolling down to rocks and the sea; sheep and goats, weathered fences, gardens. He remembers the small houses, painted bright colors or plain white or just left to darken in the elements. He remembers the Easter-basket wallpaper in his room overlooking Capelin Cove, and the saggy, creaky steel bed, and the nice musty smell—the room had not been used since November, according to its calendar, which was still open to that month. He remembers a night on the water watching a school of capelin shimmering in the moonlight, the fish breaking the surface occasionally as if being chased from below. From the moonlit capelin, he and Bora shifted their gaze to the moon, studying, through the spotting scope, the dry, bright seas there. He remembers diving, in daytime, into a sea of capelin as they bred near shore. The entire bottom was rolling with capelin eggs, and flounder were everywhere eating them. He and Bora caught one flounder and practiced their amateur science on it, opening the stomach and examining the contents, which proved half capelin eggs, half tiny green bottom stones. Bill remembers a dog he liked in Newfoundland, Moondog. He remembers steaks from a road-killed moose, cooked on a fire at the edge of the pavement. He remembers a sea meal: boiled mussels with lemon juice, fried capelin, Dominion Ale, coal-baked potatoes, Cadbury bar, Maxwell House coffee. He remembers a minke whale underwater, thirty feet away, bobbing its head in warning. He remembers another minke, rising beneath, turning slightly to bring its right eye to bear. Minke flukes became Bill's favorite, the most gracefully carved of any flukes he knows. If he ever carves a set himself, he says, they will be a minke's. He remembers that trapped humpback whale, its flukes caught in a cod net. He remembers the humpback's skittishness the first day, its resignation the second; and the companion whale that refused to abandon it, swimming distant circles around it all day; and the whale's uncanny sensitivity—when Bora touched the flukes with one gloved finger, the

great brain, forty feet away, received that tiny message, and the whale pumped its flukes as sharply as the cod net would allow. He remembers the day that rain, fog, and gale-force winds kept them ashore, letter-writing and gear organizing, and how, later that night, they went into town to see "Chesty Morgan," a pornographic murder movie, watching, alongside silent Newfoundlanders, as Chesty, the heroine, smothered her victims with her huge, balaenopterous breasts.

Should he forget any of Newfoundland, Bill has his photographs to remind him: Portraits of Newfoundland horses. Portraits of cows. Photos of cows licking salt from wetsuits spread on the bushes to dry. Night photos of driftwood fires by the Atlantic. Still lifes of various dinners-to-be; mussels laid in a row on a driftwood board, or flounder, mussels, and capelin laid on a stone—culinary Edward Westons. Fool-around photos of Bora and Kate. Bora in his wetsuit emerging from the sea, hands crooked into claws, two capelin in his mouth for fangs. Kate pouring beach pebbles on her head. Kate eating the pebbles.

Bill remembers, without recourse to photographs, the evening of the summer solstice, when gulls dipped low over the Atlantic, skimming the capelin schools gathering just out of their reach, the gulls crying not in frustration, he thought, but in anticipation, as if they knew that tonight, or tomorrow, those same unreachable capelin would be lying in silver windrows above the falling tide. He remembers the stranded corpse of a blue whale, its flanks carved with initials, like a statue of Lincoln disfigured by vandals. He remembers humpbacks feeding in the tide rip in Holyrood Bay; the incoming swells meeting turbulently the outgoing tide at the mouth of the gut, the whales spouting mistily against an orange sky, the surf roaring, the stranded capelin flip-flopping by the hundreds as the wave that had deposited them went back to fetch another silvery truckload, the odor of dead capelin rising from the windrows, the fragrance of living capelin blowing in from the sea and raising goosebumps, the humpbacks leaping, three and four at a time, halfway out of the water, their mouths open, their baleen streaming, their ventral grooves distended; then the whales blowing,

The Fin-Back is not gregarious. He seems a whale-hater, as some men are man-haters. Very shy; always going solitary; unexpectedly rising to the surface in the remotest and most sullen waters; his straight and single lofty jet rising like a tall misanthropic spear upon a barren plain.

Spotted dolphin, Hawaii

He swam the seas before the continents broke water; he once swam over the site of the
Tuileries, and Windsor Castle, and the Kremlin. In Noah's flood he despised Noah's Ark;
and if ever the world is to be again flooded, like the Netherlands, to kill off its rats, then
the eternal whale will still survive, and rearing upon the topmost crest of the equatorial
flood, spout his frothed defiance to the skies.

· · ·

Risso's dolphins, Baja California

Hump Back . . . This whale is often seen on the northern American coast. He has been frequently captured there, and towed into harbor. He has a great pack on him like a peddler; or you might call him the Elephant and Castle whale. At any rate, the popular name for him does not sufficiently distinguish him, since the sperm whale also has a hump though a smaller one. His oil is not very valuable. He has baleen. He is the most gamesome and lighthearted of all the whales, making more gay foam and white water generally than any other of them.

Humpback, Newfoundland   *Humpback whales: escort, mother, and calf, Hawaii*

*The moot point is, whether Leviathan can long endure so wide a chase,
and so remorseless a havoc; whether he must not at last
be exterminated from the waters, and the last whale, like the last man,
smoke his last pipe, and then himself evaporate in the final puff.*
— HERMAN MELVILLE

inhaling, sinking with full mouths, turning, pausing to stroke a companion, then circling seaward to begin another run. He remembers thinking there was no place on earth he would rather be.

Bill saw his first minke whale in Newfoundland. He saw his first blue, fin, humpback, and sperm whales there too. It was not always easy telling the whales apart. The local fishermen were little help, though not from lack of willingness. The Newfoundlanders were the best-hearted folk Bill has met. Every inhabitant of that glacier-rounded fiord-indented island greeted you warmly. Everyone, even the small boys, called you "me bye" or "me son." But no one was a close student of whales. The people were forever telling Bill and Bora that on this day or that the bay had been black with whales—"Yes, me bye, the bayoo she was black with whales"—but they were casual about particulars. In diving, all whales hunch themselves more or less, and for the Newfoundlanders all whales were humpbacks. "She's got a hump on her, bye," a Newfoundlander would say, puzzled at the need for finer discriminations.

The first whale he and Bora encountered in Newfoundland, on Tinity Bay, mystified them. When it first blew, it looked like a finback; then it blew again and they saw it was too small. It had a high dorsal fin and it arched its back steeply in diving. A minke? They didn't think so; its surfacing sequence was not what the book said to expect of minkes. Days later, off Little Colinet Island, the mystery cleared. They saw fin whales and humpbacks swimming together, both species on the surface simultaneously. They realized that the earlier animal had been a hybrid of their own making. That first day, a finback had dived, and moments later, farther along its apparent line of march, a humpback had risen.

Another time, searching for blue whales five miles offshore, they saw what appeared to be a blue whale surface and blow. They were primed to see a blue whale, when its spout announced it, for the weather had been poor for three weeks, and they had managed to get out on only three days in that period. Blue whale! Big as three brontosaurs. Heart as heavy as a whole horse, tongue the size of a school bus. Named *Balaena musculus*, "little mouse whale," by Linnaeus as a colossal joke. Unphotographed underwater.

Gee, that's a funny-looking blue, Bill thought, but they set off after it.

They had a passenger that day, unfortunately, and the Zodiac was too heavy to plane. It churned along, unable to catch up. A boat must travel much faster than a whale in order to get ahead and then correct for deviations in the animal's course, and the Zodiac was not fast enough. They did the best they could, motoring to the last place they saw a blow, then shutting off the outboard and waiting for the whale to blow again.

"Hey, look at the rostrum on that guy!" Bill yelled once. "That's a funny-looking whale."

A second boat joined the chase. In it was Wilson Kettle, a friend from the Newfoundland Fisheries Department who had been following their work with interest.

"That's no blue. That's a fin," shouted Wilson.

"I'll bet you a thousand dollars that's a blue whale, Wilson," Bill shouted back, not half so certain as he sounded.

They caught up with the whale. Racing alongside, looking down into the water at the whale on their left, they saw white on the jaw. A peculiarity of the fin whale is that the species is asymmetrically colored, with white markings on the right side of the jaw. "Gee, Wilson, you might be right," Bill said.

When they had gained a little on the whale, Bill rolled into the water. The whale passed, a faint shape too distant for a picture. Bill squeezed the shutter anyway, like a cavalryman taking a parting shot at Sioux. Bora retrieved Bill and they caught up with the whale again. This time, from the Zodiac, Bill took a closer look. He noted the lumpy serrations of the spine, and the shape of the caudal peduncle. The dorsal fin was not, he abruptly realized, very much of a dorsal fin. It was just a serration slightly more elevated than the others. He remembered that there was another whale besides the fin with white on the jaw.

"Bora, that's a sperm whale," he said.

The sperm whale was his first. Recalling it, Bill shakes his head. "We remembered all the blows, then. They had all been forward—a sperm whale blows forward. There we were, out with a bull sperm whale, thinking we were with a blue."

It was a real miscalculation. The blue whale, the largest of the baleen whales, is a krill-eater, a grazer. A sperm whale, the largest of the toothed whales, is a hunter in whose stomach seals are sometimes found. The sperm whale, *Physeter catadon,* is the animal that used to make kindling of whaleboats and toss Nantucketeers like toys.

"We were flipped out, for a number of reasons. One was that we'd been so blind. All the cues we had missed. There couldn't be two whales more different. We were shocked at ourselves, but delighted. We'd been in the water with a sperm whale and had almost got a picture."

In the picture he almost got, the ceiling of the ocean is wildly tilted, for he had no time to level it. Shafts of sunlight angle down, converging at some point outside the frame. Caught in the warp of the beams is an imperceptible thread of reflected light. Bill insists the thread is there, at any rate, after he has studied the slide for a while through a magnifying glass. Perhaps it is. Sometimes you think you see it, sometimes you don't. The thread of light, if it exists, is faintly suggestive of a fullness, like the thread of a new moon. It curves up toward the surface, about to blow and take a breath. This is Bill's sperm whale. It is a surpassingly marginal whale. It's a hope, a might-have-been. But it is more truly representative of the whales of his life than those rare photographs that turn out better.

Most of Bill Curtsinger's whales have been glimpses. Whales are fast and inhabit a shadowy medium. They have minds of their own, and a vast, three-dimensional ocean to wander in. More often than not, Bill gets in the water ahead of whales only to find they've changed tack and he's no longer ahead of them. When he does see something underwater, it's usually blurry and distant. As soon as he raises the viewfinder to his eye, he sees the whale at an additional remove, through the wrong end of the telescope of his wide-angle lens. The whales of his memory are mostly receding from him. His gray whale disappears into a pasture of California kelp. His killer whale, startled, lurches away into the dimness of Puget Sound. (Most of the killer-whale population of the Sound has been captured by oceanaria at one time or another, and the whales are shy, having lost the old fearlessness of the species.) His pilot whale passes him dimly with a large fish held crosswise in its mouth. It passes so dimly, in fact, that only in examining the photograph closely did Bill see that the fish's tailfin was horizontal, not vertical. The fish was no fish. It was a small cetacean—probably the pilot whale's dead calf.

The currents off Newfoundland were cold, greenish, and filled often with the protoplasm of ctenophores. Visibility underwater was seldom good. In Newfoundland

Bill saw his whales in fragments. Of one finback, he saw just the flukes, moving swiftly up and down and out of sight, glimpsed and gone within instants of his tumbling into the water. Of one humpback, he saw just the great white pectoral fins, the whale passing belly-up thirty feet below him, nothing visible but those pale, fourteen-foot oars, and even them so doubtful that at first he mistook them for the whale's open mouth. Of a second humpback, he saw just a single white pectoral fin, disembodied, with a school of dark fish outlined against it. Of a third humpback, just the white, piebald markings on the underside of the flukes. Of one minke whale, just the white bands on the pectoral fins, broad service stripes on invisible sleeves

If Bill saw his baleen whales fragmentarily in Newfoundland, they sometimes did not perceive him at all. Baleen whales lack, as far as we know, the toothed whale's echolocation apparatus. They could hear the boat passively, and always knew where it was, but sometimes they lost track of the man. Swimming slowly once toward three humpbacks as they fed on a school of capelin, Bill saw them turn unknowingly toward him. From the surface he took one last look. He saw them blow thirty feet away, and he noticed the genital slit of one whale as it rolled partway over on its back. Then he put his face mask under. The water was full of capelin, and he grabbed one that had been stunned by one of the approaching humpbacks. On came the whales. Two of them glided by to either side of him, as big as houses, and the third passed underneath. The first two were so close he could have touched them, though all he saw was the whiteness of the pectorals. Alarmed that they could be so oblivious, he slapped his hand on the surface, letting them know he was there. At least one of the whales turned back, for he saw an enormous vague outline pass under him again.

"There's no trick to it," Bill says of his technique. "It's

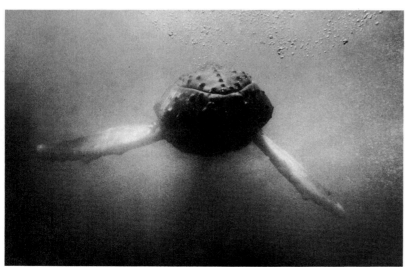

Trapped humpback nodding its head in warning, Newfoundland

trial and error. One time, Bora left me in the water and motored away. You know, trying to fool the whales. Which is absolute folly—trying to fool the whales. They're so acutely aware, because of their equipment. They know something's been dumped off. We even tried throttling down slowly, over a minute or so, to make it sound as if the boat was drawing more distant. That didn't work either.

"The biggest trick is getting out of the boat. A lot of people don't do that. I often find myself reluctant to get in the water and go off from the boat. Especially when I'm alone. You're drawn to the boat. It's like a house or something. It's just what we are; we don't belong out there. It's hard, getting in the water and having the boat go away—and it has to go away if the whales are going to come. When seas are high, the boat is usually out of sight.

"Strange waters are pretty weird. You just never know. The first few times in new waters you feel strange. Water in different parts of the world has different colors and feeling. There's bluish feeling in the Pacific—clear blue oceanic water. Newfoundland and the continental shelves are greenish.

"Once Bora lost me. Only for about ten minutes. He set up some sort of search pattern and found me—which is why I have Bora. I wasn't really nervous—he was probably more upset than I. I could see land. In Newfoundland, there was nothing going to eat me. Well, I guess maybe great whites. But the likelihood of anybody running into a great white, on the East Coast—I'd go with the odds. After that incident, we glued yellow circles of neoprene on either side of my hood, so he could see me better."

Bill is aware of the void under him, but is not troubled by it.

"I worry about dropping the camera. I think of depth

in those terms. If you drop it, it's gone. The Ocean-eye is a very special tool. It's the best housing there is, right now. You can't buy them anymore. It's just everything to me. I loop the cord around my wrist and twist it a couple of times. I always think that if I were jarred by a whale, or struck accidentally, it wouldn't fall out of my hand."

Bill's camera equipment is always changing. For surface photography in the field, he brings two working cameras and a spare. The surface camera in favor lately is the OM II, which has the automatic metering he likes best, having repeatedly tried to fool it and failed. He would like to see a good underwater housing for the OM II. Everything about picture-taking is more difficult underwater; meter-reading, knob-turning, steadying the camera, and underwater light is tricky. A system that would free him from responsibility for exposure would be a boon. For now he uses a Nikon with two or three lenses in the Ocean-eye housing.

"I bring along an extra Nikon as a back-up, and a Nikonos too. A Nikonos with a fifteen-millimeter lens is handy for marine mammals. It's super wide, and you have to be really close to things, but for *whales*, it's terrific. But the Nikon in the Ocean-eye is still the bread and butter. I bring some motor-drives and a bunch of lenses. The motor-drives on the housings are super finicky. One drop of salt water in the electric connection, and it doesn't take long to disintegrate."

At the beginning of his career, when he was with the Navy in Antarctica, Bill used flash bulbs. Lately, when available light has been insufficient, he has used a strobe, but in a recent story on tuna he tried bulbs again and liked them. In cold water, he found, the strobe recycled more slowly than he could reload bulbs.

"I've got to keep up with diving gadgets, too. I have to devote some time to it, talking to people, more than anything. But I have more junk than I need. It's just Bora and

*In no living thing are the lines of beauty more exquisitely
defined than in the crescentic borders of these flukes.*
—HERMAN MELVILLE

I, that's the thing that works. People don't understand that. They always try to enlarge it. It's just Bora and I in a tiny rubber boat. With more people you just compound the problem of logistics. Bora and I can go anywhere and do about anything. We can do it better than any two people I know."

Of their technique in Newfoundland, Bill continues:

"So you drive way around and try to get out in front of the whales. Once they go by, they're by. You can't keep up in fins. The whales are in constant motion. Once in a while, when they're courting or lovemaking, you can keep up—they're distracted by the social thing. Otherwise not. It's effortless motion—the flukes are moving stately, slowly—but the whales are doing three knots. And when they're bothered, it's amazing how fast they move the flukes and how powerfully that moves them through the water. The power is all in the flukes—that big engine on the back. I have photographs where you can see the cavitation trailing them in the water.

"It's all brief encounters. You're usually just snorkeling, without tanks. You're sort of hiding on the surface. You wait for the right moment to dive. If you go too soon, they might see you. So there *is* some timing involved.

"You're looking in the direction you last saw them from the surface, waiting to see a shape. You're looking around hard, especially if it's murky; moving your head around, trying to cover the hundred and eighty degrees in front of you. It's funny how things materialize underwater. It's like a magic trick. One moment it's not there, and a millimicrosecond later, there it is. There's no time to think aesthetic thoughts. You're looking, looking, looking for that shadow in the water."

11. Narwhal

NORTH OF BAFFIN ISLAND there was no barrier to the winds sweeping down from Greenland and the pole. The gales howled off the bay and blew the tent down. The men repitched the tent. The gale blew it down again. It was August 1975, and two weeks had passed since Bill had left the whales of Newfoundland, five months since he had finished photographing harp seals. He was here in the Canadian Arctic in pursuit of horned whales.

The camp was on a narrow gravel beach above Koluktoo Bay. The low hills of Baffin Island, all gray rock and rusty lichen, rose behind. There were no trees. A few patches of tussock grass grew along the shore.

The narwhal came by the very first morning. The eerie sound of their underwater communication carried a great distance through the air, almost as if someone had deployed hydrophones. Bill ran naked from the tent, down the gravel to the water's edge.

"It was the most uncommon, bizarre noise I've ever heard," he says. "And then here came the narwhal. They come close to the shore if they're not disturbed. They passed by, almost a parade."

Narwhal in old Norse means "corpse whale." The white mottling of the whale's body must have suggested, to old Norsemen looking for portents, a cadaver long afloat. The narwhal, like the killer whale, pilot whale, and beluga, is simply a big dolphin. The largest narwhals are sixteen feet long. Males have a tusk—a long and spiral modified tooth. It is this tusk that medieval naturalists stole from the whale and attributed to the unicorn. In the dark ages before Lister and Salk, infusions of the horn were good for scurvy, old ulcers, dropsie, running gout, consumptions, distillations, coughs, palpitations of the heart, fainting fits, convulsions, king's evil, rickets in children, melancholy or sadness, the green sickness, obstructions, and various distempers.

The narwhal is exclusively an arctic dolphin. Little is known of its habits. On that cold morning, as the narwhal parade passed and Bill watched naked from the windswept gravel, no underwater photograph of a narwhal had ever been taken.

The last narwhal blew and the procession vanished in the distance. For a week nothing moved on the water but the wind. Koluktoo Bay is huge; the horned dolphins circumnavigate the shoreline, and days pass before they come again. Weeks went by, and that first day's excitement slipped away. The weather was terrible, and on the few good days the narwhal did not cooperate. They returned again according to their circuits, but they would not let boats close. Bill tried camping on the other side of the bay, to see if the whales were more frequent there, or less timid. They were neither. He tried camping on an offshore island. The narwhal did not like the island any better. He borrowed the Zodiac of the two film-makers he was working with, but the outboard motor scared off the whales.

"A couple of times we saw the Inuit chasing narwhal," Bill says. "They use a big, long canoe with an outboard. The guy in the bow has a gun. The Eskimos seemed to chase them in front of us on purpose. They know where your sensitivities lie."

Bill soured on the Eskimos. He soured too on his colleagues. The photographer gets irritable when things go badly in the field. "I guess I'm disappointed in things too much," he concedes. "I felt they weren't putting one hundred percent into filming narwhal. I felt duped. I was always on Joe's ass about giving me the Zodiac. Stan and Joe were into pulling down their pants and mooning each other. There's that whole aspect of the diving community I can't relate to."

To be alone, Bill headed inland.

"I hiked around," he sighs. "There was a lot of cavernous-weathered rock behind our camp. That's a term I learned in Antarctica, in the dry valleys. Baffin Island was sort of a similar place. Foothilly. There was lots of geology around. It looked like a fossil hunter's dream." Bill was not a fossil hunter, of course. He was a whale photographer. He was reduced now to taking flower portraits instead. He shot rolls of bog cotton and arctic poppies, without knowing the name for either. He shot memorial photos of the stranded bones of seals and narwhal and ancient bowhead whales. The bones were overgrown with moss and lichen, stark against the stark landscape.

Finally one day, when things looked hopeless and he sensed that the others had given up, Bill put on his wetsuit. He informed them that he was swimming out. The narwhal were afraid of boats, but maybe they wouldn't mind a swimmer. He would stroke out, just hang around and see what happened.

"When I get frustrated about my work," he explains, "when things aren't happening, I always think of that line, 'Seek and ye shall find.' That trite, stupid little phrase. What it means to me is, if you're a photographer, get off your ass and walk around."

Koluktoo Bay was water, so the photographer got off his ass and swam. Beneath him the gravel bottom shelved off into rock. Then he passed through a zone of kelp. Then the bottom dropped away, and beneath him there was nothing to see. The water was cold, but not panicky cold. Bill was nervous, as always on first swimming into new waters, but the nervousness passed. There were supposed to be Greenland sharks around, a species slow and dull witted in its refrigerated home currents, yet dangerous in a sleepy way. Bill did not worry much. He has always felt safest in polar waters, for no reason he can explain. It was good to be alone. He was enjoying himself.

One hundred meters from shore, he saw an apparition.

"It was a ghostly group, but then they were gone. It's almost like a mirage, it happens so fast and vague and distant."

But it wasn't a mirage. Moments later, out of the gloom, straight from the bottom, came a male narwhal. The body was torpedo shaped, and the pectoral fins were small. The narwhal looked as if it should be solid and slow, but it maneuvered sharply and gracefully. Bill saw the morbid mottling that the Norse had noted, but the animal inside the cadaverous skin was entirely alive. The head was blunt as a sledge hammer; faceless, except for a dim eye. In the characteristic way of whales, the narwhal turned its body away to bring the eye to bear on him. With this movement, the tusk, which at first had pointed toward him, now in curiosity swung off.

Bill squeezed the shutter. For the first time ever, light from a narwhal in its element fell upon emulsion.

The first narwhal departed, giving way to other members of the pod. For a time Bill was surrounded by nothing but females. Then he saw a calf with a six-inch tusk. Momentarily he glimpsed a big animal with a tusk five or six feet long. The king of this tribe? It vanished in the depths. All the animals surprised him with their agility. They were not so maneuverable or fast as the smaller dolphins he had known—duskies or bottlenoses—but they were quick. In their mobility they reminded him of belugas.

Narwhal sound tugged at and cradled and rocked him. It was totally unfamiliar. "The most unusual I've ever heard," he says. "I've never heard a man-produced or animal-produced sound like it. It wasn't that tweety-bird sound of belugas. Narwhals are completely different—they have a different language."

There were ratchet sounds, like fishing reels unwinding. There was a noise like the cooing of doves, which plummeted to a deep, croaking roar like the call of a Micronesian pigeon—if you've ever heard one of those. Then a whistling, as if somewhere undersea a congested human, a merman, were sleeping on his back. Then the ratchet sound again. Then a groan like a tree creaking. Then an insistent noise, something like a donkey's braying. Then the trumpeting of an elephant with a very thin trunk. Then a gutteral roar like a lion's. Then a moment of quiet, as if the lion were gathering itself. Then the lion charged, scattering a flock of gulls.

The narwhal lingered while Bill exposed the last frame on the roll. He swam ashore to reload, and when he returned, the whales were still there. "They were very curious," he says. "They had no reason to stay." He pauses a moment, remembering. "It was one of the nicest gifts I've ever been given by an animal."

When it was over; when the whales were gone and Bill had stripped off his wetsuit, he walked inland. It was one of those moments in a life. He chose to share it with Baffin Island, with the island's old bones, and lichen, and cavernous-weathered rock. "I'd spent a lot of time among the lichen, because I got along better with them than with the people. So that's where I went. I like to be by myself. You think more about things and you're not distracted." Bill thought now about the narwhal. The majority had been tuskless, but not the first. *The first one was a tusked male*, he thought, full of wonder at his luck. He strolled out into the windcarved emptiness, through the bog cotton and pale poppies, and he loved it.

"I don't know why polar regions appeal to me so. I'm very comfortable in them, I really like them. And then there was the gift the place had just given me."

Baffin Island embraced him, Bill Curtsinger, the first human to greet the unicorn in its blue-green garden.

Humpback feeding, Newfoundland

12. *Elean*

JORDY GOLDTHWAITE steers *Elean* around the islet to approach from the seaward side. The landward side is a gravel beach occupied by ducks and gulls. The birds watch the passing lobster boat with suspicion, but nobody lifts off. *Elean*'s prow turns the miniature cape. The islet's seaward side has boulders, a stout sea barrier, and close to the gray rock bobs an orange snarl of lobster buoys, deposited there by last week's storm. This is the first of the tangles that Bill is to sort out for Jordy.

The lobsterman eases *Elean* as close to the rocks as he dares. He shifts to neutral, and Bill sits down to put on his wetsuit, undressing quickly under the cool Maine sky. Jordy and I look down on Bill as the T-shirt comes off. Bill's skin is white from this summer's confinement on the icebreaker, chasing walruses in the Chukchi Sea, and his face now seems ruddy in comparison. We see the shark scar on his shoulder, and Jordy politely looks away.

Bill pulls on his hood and mask, which distort his features. Through the glass of the mask, he looks hard at Jordy. "Stay right around here," he says pointedly. Jordy nods. Last time they did this together, Jordy had failed to understand the danger in leaving a diver alone in the ocean. After dropping Bill off, he had motored away to tend his lobster traps. This was admirable Maine efficiency in the use of his time, but it did not make Bill happy, and today he wants to make sure it doesn't happen again.

Jordy Goldthwaite is a shy, taciturn man of about sixty, the chief of Biddeford Pool's volunteer fire department and a part-time lobsterman. *Elean,* his boat, looks as ancient as the sea. She is as cicatrized as an old African woman, with scars and scratches all over her. She has a pre-Columbian winch, and a gaff that one of Agamemnon's sailors might have thrown once at a Trojan. Her full name is *Eleanor M.,* but time and the elements have abbreviated her.

Bill swims toward the buoys, using just his snorkel. As he swims he looks down and around him, trying to spot the buoy lines. He does not see them until he reaches the buoys themselves. Finding a line finally, he follows it a short distance to the northeast, and there he dives.

With Bill gone beneath the surface, Jordy looks away. To the south he sees five, then six harbor seals swimming our way to investigate Bill, and he points them out to me. The first seal rises up out of the water to look for Bill, wondering where he has disappeared to. "Curious, just like people," says Jordy.

Bill surfaces. He swims toward *Elean,* towing the two freed traps and their buoys. His flippers churn in low gear, for the weight and drag of the traps, line, and buoys is considerable. Jordy shakes his head. "I wouldn't have believed he could tow that," he says.

The harbor seals have followed underwater. One surfaces about twenty yards behind Bill, bounding chest-high above the water. It looks left and right for Bill a little frantically, then looks around behind, as if afraid it has overshot the human or has come up too close. Seal and man fail to see each other. The seal swims away fast to rejoin its friends. Innocent of the seals, Bill swims up and hands Jordy the line. We winch the trap up, and, as Bill treads water below us, we tell him about his recent companions. "You're kidding!" he says. We point to the proof—sleek heads now receding from us.

Jordy motors to the second snarl. This one is about a mile off Bill's house, and there are only two tangled buoys this time. They huddle together, as if still terrified by the memory of the storm. Bill uses tanks for this snarl, and he is under the surface for a long time.

While he's gone, I study the shore: the poplars and pitch pines on Bill's land, and the roofs of his house and cottage peeking above; the whitewashed Coast Guard tower; the long line of houses along the sandy ridge marking the Stretch, most of the windows boarded up; the pool, its blue paler than the ocean's. At the pool's southwestern end stands Jordy's house, the oldest in Biddeford Pool. According to local legend, the house once was attacked by Indians. Female ancestors of Jordy's gathered pumpkins from the field and piled them on the top step inside. As the Indians approached, they rolled them downstairs to make a rumble like a whole platoon of Goldthwaites descending, and the Indians departed.

Jordy knows this view too well. He has better things to do than gaze at it. While we circle the spot where Bill disappeared, Jordy busies himself repairing the storm-splintered cages of his traps. From a bundle of laths he pulls a replacement and nails it in place. He baits up, shuts the trap door, pauses momentarily to spin the helm, correcting our drift away from Bill, then he ties off the bait line on its cleat and dumps the trap back overboard. Sinking, the dark bars of the trap turn a frothy, bubbly green and disappear.

Bill surfaces and signals us over. As *Elean* comes alongside, he holds up the trapline, which Jordy gaffs and pulls aboard. "God, what a mess," says Bill. "There were two snarls, one about thirty feet down."

We motor to a third cluster of tangled buoys, and Bill uses tanks again. While he is under, Jordy busies himself emptying the traps of the second tangle. There are lobsters inside, but only one is a "keeper." He flips the undersized lobsters back in rapid succession. Some spin clockwise in the air, some counterclockwise, some with no English at all. The lobsters are not feeling very chipper, after their week in the trap, and they sink motionlessly, not one swimming a stroke.

Finishing, Jordy joins me at *Elean*'s side, and together we watch Bill's bubbles. Rafts of them rise, marking the irregular rhythm of his breathing below. There is something mildly disconcerting in the lag-time between each of Bill's breaths and our evidence of it.

"I wonder what it looks like down there?" I ask Jordy.

Jordy smiles peculiarly and looks down at the opaque, green, secret-holding surface of the ocean he has fished all his life, the ocean his family has fished since the days of Indians. "I've asked myself that many times," he says.

Fin whale jawbone, Newfoundland

13. Kona

AT QUARTER TO SIX, Bill tapped on my window. The stars were still bright in the sky. I found my glasses and looked for the Southern Cross, but it had set. To the east, over the black shoulder of the volcano, was a band of pearl-gray light. I pulled on my swim trunks and walked barefoot into the kitchen. Bill poured me coffee. He cut a papaya down the middle and pushed half my way. I took a sip of the coffee and began making our peanut-butter-and-jelly sandwiches. I bagged them and laid them in the ice chest, then filled our plastic bottles —guava juice for Bill, passionfruit-orange for me—and I stuffed those in too. Finishing our papaya and coffee, we began carrying the diving gear and cameras to the car.

It was the spring after Jordy and I had stood on *Elean*'s deck wondering what it looked like down there. I was finding out. Bill had come to Hawaii to photograph dolphins, and I was taking Bora's place as his assistant.

Bloater, the Zodiac, waited outside in the dark, lashed on top of the stationwagon. I climbed up, connected the hose of the foot-pump to a valve in the pontoon, and stomped to restore the tautness lost in the coolness of the night. As I watched, Bill, carrying an aluminum camera case, paused by Bloater's bow and bent close to examine her. He rubbed his hand over a spot where the gray neoprene had worn down to fabric. "Bloater's getting old," he said. He sounded a little shocked by the realization, and sad.

I drove us along the Kona shore. There were no headlights on the road but ours, no sound but the surf. The air, cool still but guaranteeing heat, was full of sea smell and the fragrance of things that bloom in the night. At Keauhou, I backed the stationwagon down the ramp almost to the water, then set the handbrake. We lifted Bloater off the top and carried her to the water. The cement of the ramp, grooved to provide traction for tires, felt good under my bare feet. The water, here in the subtropics, was a shock, but a very mild one.

We motored slowly until we passed the last of the moored boats, then, at the entrance to the small harbor, where we began to meet swells from the open sea, I throttled up. The ocean presented its simplest face to us in the mornings, when the swells were smooth, untextured as yet by wind. West of us the clouds were turning pink, the day's first color, and I headed there.

Half a mile out, we looked back at the penumbral island. The sun was now striking high on the southeastern slope of Hualalai, the near mountain. The low-angle light brought out the detail and relief in a small patch of mountainside. The rest of the volcano was dark. From the summit, the slopes fell away sharply at first, then smoothed into the long curve of the volcano's shoulder. While we watched, a crepuscular shaft appeared over the shoulder's edge.

Light travels straight, as nearly as the eye can tell, and in its straightness the morning beam accentuated the volcano's gentle arc. That basaltic arc, full, weighty, curving just perceptibly, occurs nowhere else in nature. It is unique to the great shield volcanoes. Hualalai's arc ran to the north, where it intersected the greater, darker arc of Mauna Loa. Mauna Loa was all arc. No peak spoiled its summit. Mauna Loa looked like a black-cinder moon, near and enormous, rising over Hawaii.

Near the midpoint of Mauna Loa's curve, a halo of sky began to glow brighter and brighter. The halo went critical and it kindled. A blip of sun appeared—a star-rise over the black-cinder moonrise. The blip was tiny, but in an instant it was too bright to look at.

We motored westward for twenty minutes, then stopped again. By now the sun had gained enough elevation that we could look east without hurting our eyes. There were details now in what had been shadow, and the island was no longer so noble. A narrow band of hotels, beach houses, and condominiums lines this stretch of the Kona coast, a littoral encrustation, like the work of some intelligent high-tidal barnacle. Our landmarks were the Kona Surf and the Kona Hilton. It was not so romantic, I imagine, as sailing from Alexandria in a dhow, or Macao in a junk. It would have been better, probably, to be Santiago setting out in his skiff from Havana. But by the time we were two or three miles out, things took their proper perspective. The human encrustation diminished with distance, the volcanic curves asserted themselves, and the island was as noble as it had ever been.

Steering, I sat on Bloater's port pontoon and watched for dolphins to starboard. Bill sat across from me, watching for dolphins to port. The morning light, as always, was hardest on our eyes. The ocean was glassy then, and the light rebounded in sheets at us. We peered into the

Humpback flukes, Hawaii

glare, looking for fins, and saw none. It had been this way for three weeks. We seldom found dolphins, and Bill had yet to take a dolphin photograph that pleased him.

The cloud cap was forming already over Hualalai. In time it would be bigger than the island. North of the summit and far below, in the middle elevations above Kealekekua Bay, someone was burning his field. The blue-gray line of smoke flowed straight downhill, for the morning land breeze was blowing. In the afternoon, the sea breeze would rise, and smoke from the same fire would flow uphill. We were three miles out, but the burned-brush smell came intermittently on the breeze.

Bill signaled me, drawing his finger across his throat. I hit the kill button, the outboard motor died, and suddenly the sea was as softspoken as it had been for the first sailors, except for a residual hum in our ears. There was a blessed moment of quiet. Then Bill took out the walky-talky. He stretched the antenna and flicked the switch. The twentieth century resumed.

When we could find no dolphins ourselves, we listened on the walky-talky to the CB conversations between fishing boats. In Hawaii, charter boats and skiffs fish on dolphins, for dolphins and tuna travel together, and the fishermen keep one another posted on the location of the schools. Today, the first accent to emerge from the static was not a skiff fisherman's pidgin, nor the laconic English of one of the white charter-boat captains. It was a deep Southern accent we knew well, for we heard it daily. After reciting his call letters, the voice always drawled, "... from the bayou country." He operated at an illegal wattage and his signal had traveled from Louisiana a third of the way around the globe. There was a babble of long-range outlaw voices like his, most of them originating in the South. We didn't like them. They had an astringent effect on planetary distances. We hated turning on the walky-talky. It instantly shrank the globe. It reminded us that this blue wilderness on which we drifted—this greatest of oceans—was invisibly polluted, that disembodied low-brow con-

versations were always skittering past us on their way to China.

Today Bayou Country's rambling discourse was cut short by the nearer, stronger voice of a fisherman. The fisherman asked his buddy, whose boat he had in sight, whether he was onto anything.

"I got a few scattered birds, but nothing's happening," the buddy answered.

"Yeah. Okay, John. Nothing here either. Hang onto a big one."

"Yep. Hang onto a biggie yourself."

The two men signed off, and Bayou Country again was audible. We listened for a minute, then Bill cursed and turned off the walky-talky. With that snap of a switch, the sea became wilderness again.

We motored closer inshore and looked for dolphins there, without success. We motored offshore and our luck was the same. We saw nothing but ocean, until Bill spotted a plastic pail, floating in the distance upside down. He asked me to detour toward it.

The pail was white, slightly cracked, and inhabited. Fifteen or twenty small fish hovered like a mobile in its shade. Bill leaned over as we came up. He snatched the pail suddenly, scooping up several fish. He studied them dourly for a minute, then poured them back over. They rejoined their friends, the other dispossessed citizens of the nation of the pail, who for shelter had gathered under the Zodiac. Bill briefly examined two tiny, blue-striped remoras stuck to the plastic, then tossed the pail back. The fish below us, in a brief fit of loyalty to their former home, streaked for it, but no sooner had they arrived at the pail than they streaked back to Bloater. They liked the boat better. The Zodiac cast a palace of shadow next to the hovel cast by their pail.

It was a bad decision. The shade always looks deeper under the other piece of flotsam. The fish had failed to see the great advantage of their pail—that it possessed no outboard motor. The Zodiac and the pail drifted far apart while Bill and I took a juice break and the fish explored their new home. Then I yanked the starter cord, we departed in a cataclysmic white explosion of bubbles, and the fish were left stranded in a shadowless sea.

That afternoon we stayed out on the ocean until the clouds turned pink again, this time to the east. The great crown of cumulus that had been building throughout the day over Hualalai turned from gold to red, then to gray. When the last light died, we headed home. On the way back, Bill said scarcely a word.

The dolphin we were pursuing was the spinner dolphin, *Stenella longirostris.* Dr. Kenneth Norris, one of the world's most prominent dolphin scientists, had told Bill that this small, long-beaked dolphin, which spins dramatically when leaping, would be a good subject, and that the Kona coast would be a good spot for photographing it. For years Dr. Norris had studied wild spinners in Kona's Kealekekua Bay, which the spinners visited daily, and he had found them unskittish and easy to work with.

We found them the opposite. The spinners, we discovered, no longer visited Kealekekua Bay regularly. Perhaps there were too many boats there now; or maybe the dolphins had had a bad experience there, since Dr. Norris's time; or maybe they simply had grown bored with the place. When we did encounter spinners in the bay, they were uncooperative. Dr. Norris had accompanied his dolphin schools in a homemade sub he called the SSSM, "submersible sea-sick machine." For passengers, it was a nauseating vessel, but the dolphins, long accustomed to fishing boats and to the idea of hulls, did not mind swimming along with it. They were not accustomed to a creature like Bill pursuing them in wetsuit and fins. They wouldn't let him close.

After a month we learned the dolphins' circuits and schedules, at least. We discovered where and when to intercept them, so we no longer had to motor around aimlessly, as on that day of the floating pail. We usually picked them up shortly after dawn, just outside Keauhou Harbor.

We hoped that the dolphins, seeing Bill daily, would grow accustomed to him. It never happened. Again and again, as he waited in the clear blue Hawaiian water, camera ready, conditions perfect, he would watch the school divide and pass around him, too dim and distant for photographs.

"They want no part of me," he said one morning, emerging from the water for the fourth time. He was wearing a small "pony" tank and a disconsolate expression. The spinners had not given him opportunity to use the tank. He flipped at the hoses to his pressure gauge and his regulator. "I try not to breathe with my mouth underwater, but all these things are banging around. I must sound like a freight train down there. I know they hear it, whether they see me acoustically or not."

But we kept trying. I would race us along, steering parallel to the course of the school, then, a quarter mile ahead, I would veer in front, shift to neutral, drop Bill off, and motor a short distance away. Standing in the Zodiac, I would keep an eye on the Day-glo orange tip of his snorkel, so as not to lose him. Onward came the dorsal fins of the school. The fins of spinner dolphins are small and triangular, sometimes slightly falcate. They glisten in the sun. When you gaze latitudinally down a traveling spinner school, it looks like a sea plow, a toothed roller in which the points of individual fins are continually emerging, turning, and disappearing to be replaced by new fins. Twenty yards from Bill, the fins would start swerving to either side. Bill was a negatively-charged particle in a dolphin-charged field, and he repelled them in a perfect circle. Beyond him the dolphins would join up again and continue on their way.

They varied their method of giving us the slip. Sometimes instead of going around, they dove under Bill and came up on the other side. We called this "submerged avoidance," in the fake scientific jargon we slipped into occasionally, in spite of ourselves. In submerged avoidance, the ranks of dolphins passed twenty fathoms and more beneath us, a host of vague, repeated shapes, like a faded pattern on indigo wallpaper.

When we were both in the Zodiac, the spinners would relent and pass near. Bill shot roll after roll documenting their surface behavior. He caught the spinning leaps, each dolphin turning impossibly tight, rapid circles on itself; the head-slapping; the tail-slapping; the spinner's spy hop, in which the long, slender rostrum comes high out of the water, and the small eyes search for you. In head-slapping, the dolphin usually smacked the water with the side of its head, but sometimes it used the back. When it tail-slapped we usually saw just the white, sputtery fountain that the flukes raised in the blue ocean, but sometimes we saw the pounding flukes themselves. Commonly the dolphins tail-slapped belly down, but occasionally they slapped belly up, and we saw the cream-white flash of their undersides.

We grew sensitive to the moods of the school. The collective spirit of dolphins is mercurial, seldom the same from one minute to the next. We often would recognize a particular mood from the experience of previous days. Several rest modes grew familiar, and several characteristic flurries of excitement—brief epidemics of leaping and speed-swimming that infected the school and quickly subsided. But each day, too, the dolphins showed us something entirely new.

We began to get a feeling for the larger movements of the school, both temporal and geographic. In the mornings the spinners hugged the shore, most often swimming along slowly. This was what, in dolphins, passes for rest. In the afternoons and early evenings, they headed seaward and began milling in great circles. These circles were, we thought, a gathering ritual; wide, social gyres of dolphins assembling for each night's offshore hunting. There were countermovements back toward shore, but the general drift was seaward. As the sun neared the horizon, excitement mounted. The dolphins spent more time at the surface, leaping more frequently, head- and tail-slapping more, occasionally coming over to ride our bow wave. Finally, when the clouds to the west were a conflagration and the sun a red signal fire on the horizon, the dolphins moved out. They thinned around us, then vanished. Spinner dolphins work a night shift. As we headed home, their wakefulness was just beginning.

When darkness comes to open ocean, the Deep Scattering Layer rises. The DSL is a living aurora, a bioluminescent horizon so teeming with squid, shrimp, and fish that sometimes, on fathometers, it appears that the sea floor itself is rising. The DSL begins its ascent at dusk, and the dolphins dive to meet it. Seven hundred feet and more beneath the surface, streaking dolphins invade the DSL, which divides, amid barrages of clicks and starbursts of luminescence, into scores of one-sided dogfights—small, intense, age-old dramas of pursuit and capture that no human will ever witness.

"What excites me," said Bill once, "is, what goes on when the lights go out? These guys have the equipment to survive at night when the predators are out. I like to imagine what's going on down there." We had to be content with imagining. The dolphins would not give us the smallest hint about what went on down there, even in the daylight. The surface shots were nice to get, but Bill did not find them satisfying. Dolphins spend a small fraction of their lives in the air. Their real world is below, and we were missing that.

With each day of bad luck, Bill got gloomier. He spoke less and less. When he found something to say, it was usually curt and unfriendly. Most of my own conversation seemed to strike him as stupid, so after a while I shut up myself. The arrival of his new eighth-inch wetsuit boosted him, temporarily. "There's something about a new skin," he said, looking down at himself in the Zodiac that day. (A diver with a new suit, like a boy with new tennis shoes,

gets a certain extra bounce.) Later, swinging his legs over the edge of the Zodiac, Bill prepared to test the suit for the first time. "Ze divairs entair ze wateur," he said, in imitation of Cousteau, and he slid overboard.

Bill's Cousteau narrative — heroic, French-accented voice-overs for the commonplace things we did on the water—was one of the ways he amused himself. Another was through an odd, nameless form of humor he had developed to a kind of height. It consisted of the endless repetition of a phrase something like a slogan. "I don't want those keeds next to my dump," for example. The real meaning was the meaningless, and the purpose, I think, was to drive me up the wall.

For a while the slogans were in Hawaiian pidgin. "Mo' bettah," Bill would say, apropos of nothing, or "Hey bruddah!" One evening ashore, at an imitation luau held at the Kona Surf, he heard a Hawaiian lady with a ukelele tell the drinking guests, with an imitation Hawaiian gusto, "Suck 'em up." The next day, on the water, he sang, "Hey bruddah! Mo' bettah, Ken? Suck 'em up."

His favorite line, "I don't want those keeds next to my dump," was something he had heard an Italian friend, Roberto, utter back in Maine. Occasionally he would experiment with it, altering the inflection. "I don't want those keeds next to *my* dump." Sometimes he even changed the words. If we had driven past Holualoa Elementary School that morning, it would work on his subconscious, and in the afternoon he would say, "I don't want those *elementary* school keeds next to my dump." But the point of the repetition was not to refine the slogan or improve it. Bill had picked the phrases because they were perfect already. They were his mantras.

The keeds-and-dump mantra gave way, in time, to Bill's favorite line from *The Grapes of Wrath*: "Tell 'em yer dong growed since you lost yer eye." This was powerful poetry, and Bill recited it in Oklahoma accents as thick as he could muster, but sometimes even the dong mantra was insufficient to cut through his gloom.

One afternoon in Kealekekua Bay, after a day of waiting in vain for the spinners, we cut the outboard and just drifted, fifty yards from shore. In the near distance stood the white pillar marking the spot where the Hawaiians killed Captain Cook. On previous days we had landed there. We had sat on the steps below the pillar and had scanned the bay with our binoculars, looking for fins. Today we just rocked in silence on the bay's mild chop. It was a gray day, and cool, but I liked it. Above us, reddish afternoon rays found their way through the overcast to fall in patches on Kealekekua's cliff. Counties and provinces of red light swept over the sheer rock, their boundaries

Humpback pectoral fin, Hawaii

continually changing. There was the sound of the wind in the palms and acacias of shore, and a surf sound from the waves tumbling on the lava. Bill stared off toward the monument to Captain Cook's murder. He was as grim as a detective trying to solve that murder now, two centuries later, all the witnesses long deceased, all the leads cold.

"Nice sounds, Billy," I reminded him. "Nice light on the cliff."

He looked at me wearily, having forgotten I was there. He paused, digesting with difficulty this latest of my irrelevant, Pollyannaish offerings. "Yes," he said, without the least conviction. "Nice sounds, Ken."

It was easy, of course, for me to be cheerful. I was just the boat-driver. It was not my responsibility to come home with photographs of dolphins, and there was plenty to keep me amused. Hawaii's waters, though often scarce of dolphins, were full of other things. Not a day passed without our seeing something entirely new to us. The new things were usually small, and were isolated from one another by long periods of time and wide stretches of empty ocean, but this served to sharpen perception of them, and appreciation.

One day we saw boobies diving in a way new to both of us—shallowly, as if chasing flying fish. All the boobies of our past experience had dived at steep angles. It may seem

a small secret for the sea to have shown us, but we did not view it that way. We had plenty of time to speculate over this new booby technique, in the emptiness after the birds were gone.

An albatross came through one day. It skimmed the swells, its great wingspan bearing lightly all the symbolism that various writers have heaped there. We never saw another.

One day we watched a long-tailed tropic bird dive, take a two-foot needle fish, rise clear of the water, shake its tail, scattering droplets from the long white quill, and then beat over the water, somehow maintaining its balance against the swinging pendulum of the fish.

There was flotsam and jetsam. We passed three or four floating objects each day—pails, fish floats, logs, Styrofoam ice chests. Each had its population of fish and crustaceans. Each made a distinct world, as different from the one before it as Uranus is different from Neptune. One log was a small Serengeti. Its underside was mossy with a savannah-colored sea growth. Three pilot fish swam under it, striped in black and white, like zebras. There was a herd of smaller fish, hide colored, like wildebeests. There was a third species as tawny as lions. "Africa," we agreed, on coming to the surface. A second piece of flotsam, a fish ball, had become a nation of crabs. A third was a nation of barnacles.

There were whales. *Megaptera novaeangliae,* the humpback whale, breeds in Hawaiian waters, and few days passed without our seeing several. Usually it was the flukes we spotted, as the whales made their terminal dives. At a distance, the flukes all looked dark, but when the whales sounded near us, we could see their piebald markings. These white, mottled patterns, on flukes or pectoral fins, distinguish individual humpbacks as surely as fingerprints distinguish us. Sometimes the whales breached, leaping partway or entirely out of the water. We were usually an instant late in seeing the whale rise, but just in time for the splash. It was easy to miss the dark form rising. It was hard to miss the white explosion of the return, for a playful humpback hits the ocean like a locomotive going off a bridge. It raises a whole topography of foam, mountains and valleys of it.

Hours passed, sometimes days, between these snowy disappearances. A hundred or a thousand swells would roll under us, raising the Zodiac high, then dropping it in the trough, each swell washing its predecessor from our recollection. Then, out of the corner of the eye, the glassy forward slope of a swell would erupt mountainously, fixing that particular swell's shape forever in memory.

When we turned in time to see the whale itself, we could

never quite believe its size. It seemed to rise in slow motion and it was forever coming out. Humpbacks usually emerge doing half twists, their fourteen-foot pectorals flopping in great arcs, sheets of spray whipping centrifugally away.

"Can you believe that?" Bill shouted after one nearby breach. "Can you believe that?" The breaching whale, a mother with calf, made two spy hops, coming halfway out of the water, then she moved off.

More calmly now, Bill said, "It's very unusual, a humpback breaching that close to shore. I've never seen that before—only with gray whales. It makes you realize how little we know about behavior. That was a mother with a calf. What was she doing? Instructing the calf in some way? Disciplining it? Or responding to some acoustic signal ten miles away? Or just playing?"

The blows of the humpbacks were like grenades going off. One moment there was blue sky, the next moment the cloud was there, full blown. That first, faster-than-the-eye expansion of vapor and water, leaving the blowhole at four hundred miles per hour, looked like white light. It could have passed for a primary source of photons. Sometimes, when the whale blew in bright, low-angle daylight, the spout for a millisecond held a spectral scatter of color, as if the whale's lungs had been bursting with atomized rainbows. The color instantly shimmered out, the spout frayed at the edges and turned into mist. After a lag the sound arrived, like a distant gunshot.

The spout's character changed with wind conditions. On most of this leeward coast, the spout was vertical and the mist hung in the air for a long time. Above Kawaihai, though, where the trade winds veered over the island's low northern tip, the blows were bent nearly horizontal and the mist was quickly erased.

On some days we saw no humpbacks but heard their voices. *Megaptera novaeangliae* of all whales is the greatest singer. Roger Payne, Bill's cetologist friend from Patagonia, believes that solitary males do the singing. Dr. Payne has evidence that all the humpback bulls of a given region sing variations on the same song, and that the song changes each year. Because water transmits sound so well, and because the humpback's instrument is so powerful, the songs carry tens of miles, sometimes hundreds. In the pristine ocean, before the seas were polluted by propeller sound, the singing must have carried thousands of miles, thinks Dr. Payne. One hot afternoon, on a day we saw not a sign of whales, we went into the water to cool off and heard them clearly. There were passages of regal trumpeting, then passages of bass groans. Occasionally the whale's voice was so loud and immediate it startled us. We jerked around, expecting to see the whale looming behind us. The whale, in fact, was ten miles or more away. We came to accept this consciously—that sound traveled differently in this medium, that the voices here were larger—but we could not recalibrate our reflexes. The next time a snatch of song came, we jerked around again.

One morning we rolled into the water a quarter mile from a solitary whale. It was singing, its voice so loud we heard it with our feet and hands. We crawled hand over hand down the anchorline, stopped eight feet under, and listened until our breath gave out. We returned for air, then crawled down to listen some more.

Later, back in the Zodiac, we realized we were still hearing the song. It was so faint as to be doubtful at first, but then we were sure of it, both the high notes and the low. If ever there was a spirit voice, it was that one; inhuman, originating somewhere in the waves, borne briskly toward us on the sea wind.

And there were other sorts of whales.

One day, seven miles offshore, we saw something big and distant on the water. "That's no humpback," said Bill. I sensed, too, that this was something new. For one thing, we were farther out than humpbacks liked to go, in this season. And the whale was too small. It was just lying on the surface, unhumpbacklike. It had a reddish tint that humpbacks didn't. We motored to within fifty yards, and the whale dove. It was, we agreed, about the size of a minke whale. Bill guessed it was a Cuvier's beaked whale.

He pulled on his wetsuit and fins and readied his camera. We waited where the beaked whale had sounded, in the remote chance it would rise near the same spot. The sea was calm. If the whale surfaced anywhere within the radius of a mile or two, we would see or hear it. The water was clear. If the whale should rise right here, we could watch it coming from a long way down.

After half an hour, Bill looked at his watch. "He's been down thirty minutes! Can you imagine what that animal is doing down there?" We sat in the Zodiac, peering into the deep blue and trying to imagine.

For a beaked whale, diving, that blue shaded rapidly into black. The pressure grew inexorably. Lungs collapsed, heart and metabolic rates slowed, and the whale began asking the blackness its sonic question. "Are you there, squid?" it clicked, in rough translation. "*Are you there, squid?*" came the echo-answer.

Did the squid, a mile deep in total blackness, have any sense that the whale was coming? As the sonic probes penetrated its tissues, was there a tingling, a malaise, a brief moment of premonition? Or was the squid's first intimation of its death the shock of the whale's pressure wave, and an instant later the pain of the peglike teeth?

And the whale. How did it keep its orientation down there? How, after catching its squid in the darkness, did it know which way was up?

We could not wait any longer. We were after dolphins and we had to return to that search. We motored northward and farther out, and there, an hour later, we came upon Cuvier's beaked whale again, this time a group of four of them. They rolled slowly at the surface, hyperventilating after a deep dive. Three of the whales were a reddish gray-brown, like the earlier beaked whale, and one of those three had a creamy mottling on its head. The fourth and largest whale was an albino. It had a little pigment in its dorsal fin; otherwise it was white.

We were excited. An underwater photograph of a beaked whale, and an albino at that, would have been a first, a coup for Bill on the order of his narwhal.

The four whales took a short, fifteen-minute dive, then resurfaced in a group several hundred yards from where they had disappeared. They spent several minutes catching their breaths, with the albino slowly rolling and blowing in the midst of the others. The albino was much bigger than its fellows. We wondered whether, in the society of the beaked whale, as with the other large toothed whale, the sperm, it was customary for big bulls to travel in harems of smaller females. We didn't know. The Cuvier is a rare, little-studied whale; it was possible that no one knew. Was the albino's lack of pigmentation a big disadvantage under the tropical sun? We didn't know that, either. The whales dove again, and this time we lost them.

We waited for a while, then gave up. Bill ceased scanning the horizon. He had been straddling the starboard pontoon in his flippers, with one leg trailing in the water. He left the leg there; he was not ready yet to go. He seemed to be listening for something. After a moment he cupped his hands to his mouth and called, in a keening whisper,

"Have youuu seeeenn the whiiite whaaaale?"

He waited, hands cupped, as if for the ghost of some Nantucketeer to answer. No answer came, but he seemed satisfied.

Suddenly he was in no hurry to leave this spot. It puzzled me. Bill's dedication to our fruitless search for dolphins burned hot and cold in cycles I never learned to predict. We had failed to photograph beaked whales, but we had got near them. This time, apparently, nearness was enough.

We happened to be in one of those patches of sea full of tiny floating life, and Bill, leaning over Bloater's side,

pushed his mask underwater to watch it pass. I followed his lead, lying on Bloater's hot, tight, gray pontoon and pushing my mask under.

It was like pushing an electron periscope into a microcosm. The ocean might have been one of those drops of pondwater crowded with simple organisms, except that here the microbes gravitated to one pole—the surface. They drifted in a gauzy layer just under the ceiling of the ocean. The winds and currents, we had discovered, were great sorters, segregators. One hour we might drift through pastures of gelatinous spheres—egg cases of some sort, floating by the billions in the ocean's top eighteen inches, all of them the same. A region of empty ocean would pass, then we would drift through acres of protoplasm with a different structure, this time a double disk. And the next hour we would see something else. Sometimes everything was mixed together, a translucent soup of small coelenterates, crustaceans, larvae, baby Portuguese men-of-war with gas bags the size of thumbnails. But today things were segregated, and right now it was the gelatinous spheres.

Bill saw something and shouted, his mouth still mostly underwater.

"Look, look, look *burble-bub-burble* look, look! *Burble burble* that pilot fish is eating that *burble* ctenophore!"

He was as excited as if a great white shark were rising under us. The drama, in fact, was much smaller and closer at hand.

Moments later he was calm. He scooped up one of the gelatinous spheres. Lifting his head from the water, he put the sphere in his mouth, rolled it around on his tongue and crossed his eyes comically. Then he spit the sphere gently back to sea and plunged his head underwater again.

Any ship that had come upon us then, two men sprawled on a small rubber boat with our heads in the sea, would have taken us for castaways and victims of the sun. Our friends ashore would have known better. They would have known that lack of dolphins finally had driven us mad.

Humpback flukes, Hawaii

14. The Blue Water

BILL GAVE UP trying to photograph the spinners. He decided to go offshore instead and try his luck with spotted dolphins, *Stenella attenuata,* the day-feeding, deepwater animal the Hawaiians call *kiko.* With that decision our fortunes changed. We hired a Hawaiian friend, Chris Newbert, and Chris's Boston whaler. The Boston whaler was larger and faster than Bloater, carried more fuel, and gave us more range. We began regularly working what Bill called "the Blue Water," the mile-deep ocean far out from shore. I now accompanied him in the water, carrying the long bangstick while he carried the short one, for this was the country of big pelagic sharks. Chris Newbert, who is a free-lance underwater photographer, often joined us with his camera.

Bill told us we would find the blue water strange, and he was right. Chris and I were accustomed to diving where there was a bottom and something to see—reef, kelp forest, fish. Here there was nothing but blue. We hung from our snorkels over a blue, infinite vault. Sunlight shafted downward, illuminating nothing. There was nothing to establish scale. The bright, blurry speck of a ctenophore a foot from your face mask, in that fraction of a second it took your eye to focus, left you startled and in doubt. We loved the blue water—it was as beautiful, in its simplicity, as any earthly desert—but we felt its spookiness too. The blueness pulsed with the things that might come out of it.

Bill encouraged our imaginations. "Every time I look at you guys, you're looking around," he said the first day. "And that's good. That's what we've got to keep doing. It's Predatorville out here. One day you'll turn around and there's going to be a big guy sitting behind you. It's going to happen. We've just got to be ready." He spoke from the authority of his shark-damaged shoulder, and we listened.

Our luck turned on the fifteenth of March. We headed far south that day, leaving behind the coastline of hotels and condominiums, working the wilder waters off the flows at Milolii. Late in the morning, four miles offshore, we saw a single strange fin. It did not belong to *Stenella*

attenuata, the species we were after, but to something else. We slipped into the water ahead of it.

We waited, our masks underwater. Converging beams of sunlight shafted down, illuminating nothing. Then, from down deep, out of the blue, came an unknown dolphin. It was solitary, which was rare with dolphins, and its species was a mystery to us. Big and gray, with a white-scarred back, it was homely as dolphins go, but homely in a pleasant, Lincolnesque way. The white scars looked honorable. I was behind Bill underwater as the two came together; the dolphin, curious, nosing up from below, Bill and his camera nosing down to meet it. Ten feet apart, they stopped. The beak probed the glass of the camera dome; the dome blinked back. The dolphin, satisfied, moved on. It was the first time I had seen a wild dolphin underwater. I can't convey the emotion of the moment, the improbability and beauty of the meeting, the two mammals somehow finding each other in that blue emptiness.

This was, we learned later, *Steno bredanensis,* the rough-toothed dolphin. Its arrival signaled the beginning of our good times. Shortly after it left, we spotted a school of kiko dolphins, maneuvered in front of them, and rolled into the water. We swam just beneath the undulating surface, peering in the direction we had last seen the dolphins from the boat. Kiko dolphins have white-tipped beaks, and it was this feature we saw first. White dots appeared in the sunlit, pale-blue water close under the surface. Then bodies materialized, coursing along behind the dots. The dots swung back and forth laterally as the beaks scanned for us sonically. The dots seemed to repel one another. One animal would swing its beak sideways until its cone of sound encountered the cone emanating from its neighbor, then the beak would bounce away, so as not to mingle signals—or so it seemed. This deference of one dolphin for the next, if that's what it was, gave the school of dots a counterweighted, calliope sort of motion. Each dolphin had an acoustic look at us from a slightly different angle.

The dolphins dove shallowly, leveled off at fifty feet, and began ascending toward us, their flukes pumping easily. In the magnification of the water, they looked bigger than they did on the surface, and paler, and much more numerous. I realized that the fins visible atop the ocean at a given moment give a small idea of the size of the school beneath.

The dolphins seemed as sudden as magic. Empty a moment before, the blue void was now full of fast, graceful, weightless legions. Some pumped straight by, glancing at us quickly as they passed. Others ceased swimming forty feet away and glided close by, turning to take stiff-necked looks. Were the cervical vertebrae fused to provide more swimming power? I thought I remembered reading that. Such a fusion seemed likely, from that limited movement of the head. Passing by, the dolphins had a way of turning their torsos away from us, twisting slightly in the region of the waist to bring one eye to bear. The movement looked slightly apprehensive, but it may have been just mechanical necessity.

The eye was the one dolphin feature that was not beautiful. Dim and pouchy, it did not catch your attention the way the clear eye of a hawk would, or of a cat, or of a human, or of any of the other creatures that really depend on sight. The eye is not the focus of a dolphin's face. It's not the best window into the dolphin's soul, if a dolphin has one of those.

A third wave of dots appeared, became dolphins, and passed, this time to our left. Pump, cease pumping, glide, twist, look, accelerate again. Most of the kikos had circular scars the size of silver dollars on their flanks. We had seen these scars earlier on spinner dolphins, but the kikos had more of them. They were the mark of *Isistius brasiliensis*, the cookie-cutter shark, an eighteen-inch, luminescent inhabitant of the Deep Scattering Layer. The small shark mimics a squid, one theory goes, which allows it to get close to the dolphin. At the last instant, it darts toward the dolphin, sinks a circular row of teeth into the dolphin's side, and tears off a disk of skin and blubber. Life in the sea, the scars attested, was not all leap and gambol. Most of the kikos had at least one scar, and many had two or three. Some of the wounds were fresh red. Most had healed white.

Remembering that there was a third dimension here, I looked straight down. A squad of dolphins, six or seven of them, were passing below. Beneath that group was another, fifteen or twenty animals so deep they were ghosts. On the animals of the upper tier, I could see the streamlined, flamelike markings. The kikos were painted more like fighter planes or hotrods than like animals. The pattern seemed intended less as camouflage than as an accent on speed—pure vanity on the part of the Designer.

Bill and Chris, following one group of dolphins, had dived to twenty-five feet, their cameras presented before them like offerings. When the dolphins moved out of range, both men glanced quickly upward to see where the surface was. I would see that upward glance often in the next weeks. The two photographers were so intent on the dolphins that they were uncertain how deep the dolphins had taken them.

Looking up, I saw that a new wave was upon us. These dolphins flew by very close, and the boldest in their curiosity came closer than they realized. When it dawned on them how near they were, they shied away suddenly. Shying, the kikos reminded me of frightened horses, their eyes rolling away faster than their heads were able.

I saw Bill swing his camera on line with a dolphin rising toward him. The dolphin silently chattered at him, opening and closing its mouth in what was clearly a threat. Bill didn't seem the least alarmed, and somehow neither was I.

I looked for Chris. He was behind me, two dolphins approaching him so closely I was sure he could touch them. The same thought struck Chris, for he reached out in a half-stroking, half-waving gesture. The dolphins shied from his hand, accelerating with several sharp strokes in perfect, uncanny unison. Each emitted, simultaneously, a thin stream of bubbles. They ceased swimming at exactly the same instant and glided side by side under the hull of the Boston whaler. They looked like a pair of cropdusters, twin contrails of bubbles marking their paths.

Spherical clusters of bubbles were rising from below, marking interactions between dolphins too deep for us to see. Things were going on down there that we could only guess at. The bubble spheres were so slow in ascending that they seemed to hang. They glimmered in the muted light, like crystal chandeliers in a blue hall.

A dolphin defecated on the move, leaving behind it a gray, cloudy stream, which the action of the flukes beat into a wavy line. Long after the dolphin was gone, the gray line hung there, like smoke after the fireworks.

A dolphin school leaves its spoor in the ocean. The bubble spheres linger, along with those erratic skywriters' lines of defecation. Fifteen seconds after the school has gone, the evidence remains, but thirty seconds afterward, the bubbles of old arguments have risen to the surface and fizzed away, the gray liquid residue of yesterday's squid has dispersed in the blue, and the ocean is trackless again.

The last dolphins were passing unhurriedly to one side of us. One dolphin left its fellows, swam up slowly for a breath, as it must have done a million times before in its career, then continued on its way. Suddenly it all felt sad. For a moment the dolphin life seemed enormously weary

Spotted dolphin (kiko), Hawaii

and Sisyphean. I thought of the endless travel through the monotonous blue void— that endless need to rise and respire, which banished true sleep as other mammals know it.

I remembered, then, all the things we had seen in our weeks on the water; the birds, the fish, the flotsam. In a single day, a dolphin saw at least as much, and at night, at depth, it saw things we never dreamed of. Still, the dolphin's scene, as Earthly scenes go, was scarce of features. I thought I understood what dolphins must mean to one another, not just for group vigilance when resting, or for teamwork in the hunt, or even for intelligent companionship, but simply as objects in a world poor in objects.

We pulled ourselves back into the boat. "Gee," said

Bill, "they might be from another planet, you know? They're so alien." We pulled off our fins, all three of us happy. It's wonderful the difference a little success makes. We shook hands all around and headed home.

For the next month we were with the kikos almost every day. Our system was to head offshore from three to twelve miles, then cruise north or south, looking for a gathering of skiffs. Chris had built a console for the wheel of the Boston whaler, and this proved a big advantage over Bloater. It gave us three extra feet of elevation, effectively moving the horizon back. We took turns standing on top, holding the painter for balance and scanning the sea. When we saw the skiffs, a cluster of specks on the horizon, we

Schools of porpoises and blackfish are only more animated waves
and have acquired the gait and game of the sea itself.
—THOREAU

turned that way. The Boston whaler was fast, and the skiffs rapidly grew larger.

Before we could make out individual Hawaiian fishermen, we saw the white splashes of leaping dolphins. We slowed a little, so the whaler would not sock the waves so hard, and we quickly pulled on our wetsuits. Usually we wore just the tight overalls of our Farmer Johns, but if the day was cool, we added our jackets. Once or twice Bill used the pony tank; otherwise we used just masks and snorkels. On reaching the school, we followed the example of the skiffs, racing ahead of the dolphin line of march, turning in front, cutting the motor, and waiting.

The Hawaiian fish by "dropping stones." The fisherman baits the hook and wraps the hook end of the line several times around a chunk of lava. Then he lays a piece of fish on top of the stone, secures it with several more turns of line, lays on another piece of fish, secures it, and so on. Unwinding underwater, the stone lays out a chum line, which the tuna follows toward the hook. Where the Hawaiians dropped their stones overboard, we dropped ourselves.

We waited in the boat until the fins were almost upon us, making sure the school would not pass to either side. Bill sat with the big Ocean-eye camera housing in his lap, his mask pushed up on his forehead. Chris adjusted his own camera, and I slipped my hand through the wrist loop of the bangstick. The wait was joyful and intense. "Here they come," one of us almost always said. Those words, and the advancing fins, the shining backs, the leaps, the spray, the explosive breaths, never failed to excite us. We pulled our masks in place and rolled into the water.

Sometimes we found the dolphins before the skiffs did, and we had them to ourselves for a while before the fishermen arrived. More often, one or another of the fishermen had made the discovery. We tried to keep some distance between ourselves and the skiffs, but occasionally we dove close enough to see the undersides of the hulls, with the fishlines at steep angles underneath.

When the skiffs started up, speeding away to drop fresh stones ahead of the school, the outboards made a lethal underwater whine. The noise seemed too high pitched for an engine, and we always wondered momentarily what it was. Then we remembered. We looked quickly around, making sure the propeller wasn't bearing down on us. Human hearing is not directional underwater, so we had to find the source—the streak of bubbles from the prop—with our eyes. If the whine bothered the dolphins, they did not let on. We sometimes saw them swimming easily in the wake of a speedboat, outlined against the white froth.

The dolphins, we learned quickly, were far less interested in us than we were in them. It would be a bitter lesson for Dolphin Embassy, we thought, or for anyone else who sought to establish diplomatic relations with wild dolphins. Sweeping toward us, the school was almost always curious, but having passed, they forgot all about us. There was one exception, a single large kiko that one afternoon circled back three times to look us over. We knew it was the same one; it was an unusually marked animal, with a beak entirely white and a remora attached between its pectoral fin and its invisible ear, like a close advisor. It was the scientist of its tribe, the Roger Payne or Kenneth Norris, and its interest in us was unusual. From time to time in history there have been dolphins like it, animals with an affinity for humans—Pelorus Jack, for example—but these animals are eccentrics. They are outside the mainstream of dolphin culture. Most dolphins have better things to do. "The proper study of dolphinkind," their philosophy seems to run, "is dolphin."

Bill told us that he observed much more once the kikos were past. This was partly a professional dilemma, for as the kikos approached, Bill's world was bounded by the viewfinder, and he was worried about focus, exposure, and earning his bread. Once the dolphins passed by, he could just watch them. Yet it was partly, too, the dolphins. When we were in front of them, they were curious, and there is not much variety in dolphin curiosity. They just swim over to see who these ungainly creatures are. But the moment each dolphin passed through the vertical plane we occupied, its attention shifted ahead, and it went back to

The hunting of dolphins is immoral, and that man can no more draw nigh to the gods as a welcome sacrificer nor touch their altars with clean hands, but pollutes those who share the same roof with him, who willingly devises destruction for the dolphins. For equally with human slaughter the gods abhor the death of the monarchs of the deep.
—OPPIAN

the things it had been doing. Sex resumed, if that's what had been going on. We never saw the act itself, but we saw foreplay. Once I watched a kiko show the white of its underside as it swam along upside down, its consort swimming above it. The upper animal stroked the whiteness near the genital slit of the lower animal with six or seven rapid jerks of a pectoral fin. The lower animal ceased to swim, or the upper animal accelerated slightly, so that the tip of the pectoral trailed forward along the whole length of the belly, grazed the chin, then ran off.

Nursing resumed. We saw the white of small bellies as the calves rolled partway over to nose at their mothers and attach themselves. Play resumed. Once Bill saw a kiko emit three bubbles down deep, chase them up to the surface, and spear each bubble in turn with its beak. I heard Bill's strangled underwater bellow as he shouted for us to look, but I turned too late to see.

One day the foreplay, or whatever it was, ran particularly hot and heavy. On the surface the kikos were milling —not heading in any special direction—and we estimated that there were a couple of hundred of them. We saw white bellies flash at the surface—always a signal that something out of the ordinary was going on. From the boat we saw several dolphins elevate their flukes above the water and wave them in the air. Were these females avoiding suitors? We could not tell. On entering the water, we saw a tight group pass under the bow of the Boston whaler, traveling as slowly as we had ever seen kikos travel. They were preoccupied and scarcely noticed us. As we watched, two pairs of dolphins, holding themselves vertical in the water, began a spinning ballet. They pirouetted up together, two

by two, toward the surface, one animal in each pair blowing bubbles. The bubbles emerged not in streams, but as five or six big silver boluses of air. The movement was formal. It seemed part dance, part chase, part threat. We had never seen anything like it and would not see it again. The dancers dissolved in the blueness before we could make sense of their steps. It was often like that. We were always too slow in the water to see the conclusion of anything. It was frustrating. We sensed that if only we could only swim a little faster, the pieces of the puzzle would fall into place.

One gray day we found the kikos off the Milolii lava flows. They were behaving strangely, milling fast in a small area. There was a large number of animals, not divided into groups, or waves, as usual. When we joined them underwater, they made fast, aggressive pass-bys. Some jawed at us, silently, in the most common dolphin warning, and one or two assumed a serpentine threat posture, rostrums pointing at us, bodies arched in an S. Others just flew by close, ratcheting us. The sonic probes were louder than usual.

When a nearby dolphin ratchets you, you hear it less than feel it. The *tik tik tik tik tiktiktiktiktiktiktiktiktik tik tik tik tik tik tik tik tik* bounces around inside your skull and mastoid process more than in your ears. This day, one probe popped so loudly inside my cranium that I knew a dolphin must be right behind. I turned in time to see two big kikos peeling off. That was, I thought, a hell of an X-ray of the brain of Kenneth Brower. I felt undressed.

Bill saw the two dolphins fly at me, and later, in the boat, said, "Gee, it would be great if we could get a picture

Kikos, Hawaii

of one biting you. We'd send it to Dolphin Embassy." I laughed. Bill thought a moment, then added, "I don't believe we'll ever get bitten, though. If we do, it won't be serious—nothing like a shark. Just a nip. Experimental."

Chris, watching the departing school, murmured, "I can't believe how their moods change."

"They're schizoid," I said. "Multiple-personality dolphins."

"We'll treat them," said Bill. "We'll start Dolphin Clinic."

The kikos often threatened boat bottoms, we had noticed. Passing under a skiff or under the Boston whaler, they would clap their jaws at it, one animal after another, sometimes coming as close as a foot or two from the hull. This was a minor revelation. Seen from the surface, kikos always seem neutral about boats, sometimes even friendly, coming over to ride the bow wave or to surf in the wake. Perhaps the whine of the outboards gets on their nerves after all. Perhaps they remember occasions when Hawaiian fishermen poison them for stealing baits. In my own opinion, there is a bravado in this intimidation of hulls. Hulls don't fight back, after all, and there isn't much risk. The threats to hulls were more absent-minded and relaxed than the threats to us.

One time, slipping overboard on the port side, I crossed under the hull to join Bill and Chris, who had slipped in from the starboard. Passing under, I saw that the dolphins were around us already, that Bill was trying to photograph a big kiko coming my way. I stayed where I was, so as not to spoil the picture, hanging inverted under the hull, my

Kiko calf backslapping to dislodge remora

butt lowermost, like a spider on a ceiling. The big kiko saw the opportunity to bluff two bottoms at once. It looped up at me, its jaws open. I saw the white inside its mouth and the slight serrations along its beak. Bill, watching, thought *This time he's going to get bit,* or so he told me later. Somehow I wasn't worried. I grinned around the mouthpiece of my snorkel at the scene I knew we made, the kiko and I.

The dolphin threat I remember best came one hazy day off the Milolii lava flows.

This day, again, the kikos showed us something new. Usually dolphin groups passing eighty feet or more beneath us were not the least interested in us. They never looked up. All we ever heard from those deep, shadow ranks of dolphins was the whistling of their routine conversation, never the clicks of their investigations. Today, for some reason, all the deep dolphins were curious. Group after group rose to look us over. One wave rose in wing formation, eighty dolphins or so—the biggest, tightest phalanx we had ever seen. Bill, looking through his fifteen-millimeter lens, could fit them all in the frame. Then, moments later, from another rising group, almost as large, five big kikos detached themselves simultaneously. They flew up at me in perfect formation, five abreast. They were as flawlessly synchronized as the Blue Angels and they emitted a buzzing, ascending banshee shriek that I can't

describe. Forty feet away, they simultaneously assumed the serpentine threat posture, letting their momentum carry them at me, but with terrific velocity still, their flukes locked in a flaps-up position, if I remember right—it's hard to be sure, because it all happened in less than three seconds. At the last instant they peeled off, and I saw the simultaneous flash of five white bellies, like petals of a flower opening, as they shot by me on all sides.

It was absolutely terrifying, I could see, yet I was not terrified. If I had been a shark, I think, I would have climbed out of the ocean and learned to breathe air. Instead of being scared, I was moved.

I don't know why my reaction was so inappropriate. It may have been that I really believed, deep down, all the literature I had read about dolphins being friendly. It may, too, have had something to do with my being so out of place in the ocean. A human is not a real combatant in the undersea wars. He's an official with the Red Cross. If sharks knew how easy it would be to eat humans, they would eat us all the time. Humans, fortunately, are not a traditional shark food item, and sharks are big on tradition. So are dolphins. If dolphins held any old grudges against humans, they would not break off those banshee charges. So swimming in the dolphin school was like having no corporeal existence. It was like being at the movies. Seeing the five kikos come at me was like riding the roller-coaster in Cinerama—my stomach turned, but I knew I wouldn't get hurt.

If a dolphin had emerged from the movie to ram me or bite, of course, my confidence would have felt foolish and misplaced, but it never happened, and here I am intact to theorize today.

With each dive, there came a time when, looking around for the next dolphin, we saw no more. A last calf pumped by, hurrying to catch up with a squadron of wraiths. The calf became a wraith itself, then disappeared. Bill, Chris, and I turned a slow circle on the unicycles of our fins, looking for a tardy wave of kikos. Nothing greeted us but three hundred and sixty degrees of blue.

If it was early in the day, Bill usually was anxious to catch up with the school again, and we swam quickly to the boat. I enjoyed the sprint back. When I ducked my head to check the water behind, the upside-down view of us always stirred the boy in me. Looking through the bright arcs of bubbles churned downward by my fins, I saw Bill and Chris, their own fins laboring behind. My buddies were foreshortened from this vantage and they looked super-shouldery. We were three masked men. We looked like comic-book heroes. If a sea was running, the trough of a swell might cut my wingmen off from view for several seconds, but they appeared again, indomitable.

Our ritual on reaching the boat seldom varied. I hovered at the side, watching underwater while Bill slipped his hand free of the wrist loop of his camera. Magnified by the water, his forearm looked like Popeye's. If the day was cool, his goosebumps were monumental. Handing me the camera, he glanced at my hand to make sure I had a firm grip. If we dropped the Ocean-eye here, it had a mile or two to sink, and no one would ever see it again but fishes. Beneath this blue was abyssal black—a perfect hell for a camera, totally without light. When he saw that I had it, Bill hauled himself, kicking, out of the ocean. The surface might have been a door to another universe. His head and shoulders disappeared through it, then his legs, and he was gone.

Once in my hands, the camera always hypnotized me for a moment.

Machinery looks better underwater. Seen through the blue filter of the Pacific, and magnified by it, the optically correct curve of the glass dome, and all the intricate clockworks within, looked unnaturally clear yet mysterious. It was as fascinating as any biological eye. I could understand why sea lions and dolphins always stared at it.

I passed the Ocean-eye up to Bill, dropped my bangstick into the boat, and kick-pulled myself up on the whaler's side. I balanced a moment, leaning in, and the front of my Farmer Johns, bosomy with water, spilled on the deck. Then I swung a leg over. Chris passed his camera up and followed himself. One of us started up the outboards, and we roared after the dolphins again.

On occasion, though, Bill was in no hurry to chase them. Sometimes after the last dolphin had left us in the water, Bill would just invert and hang upside down for a moment, taking a break and enjoying the weightlessness. He might porpoise slowly toward the boat in a modified underwater butterfly. Sometimes, looking for trailing dolphins and seeing none, he would fold into a fetal ball around his Ocean-eye and let himself sink. He went down and down, until I thought he had gone too far. Professional divers, like cetaceans, are capable of bradycardia, and their hearts can slow during dives to beat at fifty percent of the rest rate; maybe Bill was conserving oxygen that way. At last the ball of Bill unfolded, first his legs emerging, then arms, and he kicked up easily to the surface, towing the camera by the wrist strap.

One time, sinking fetally, he saw me looking down at him. His hand came out of the ball to give me a small, sad, good-bye wave. I waved back. At what I would have guessed to be twenty-five feet, he checked his depth gauge. Abruptly he came out of the ball and kicked up.

"That was forty feet," he said, in wonder. We recalibrated our visual depth gauges. The Hawaiian water was clearer than either of us had thought. I could have read the time on his watch down there. Those ghost columns of dolphins had been passing far deeper than we had estimated.

Bill had a knack for shifting focal length quickly. Once the dolphins were gone, we often spent a moment looking for smaller things in the water, and Bill was usually the first to find them. Sometimes I puzzled over what he was pointing at, then realized the thing was not distant. It lay just beyond the tip of his finger; a larval fish, a crimson shrimp, a gelatinous creature of unknown identity.

The humpback whales were thinning out now, for the breeding season was ending. We still saw humpbacks occasionally, and if they were nearby we visited. One day, five miles offshore, we sighted distant spouts and headed there. It was odd to see humpbacks so far from shore, but we didn't think much about it. Drawing near, we saw the whales in profile against the background of the lava flows. It struck us that these humpbacks were spending an inordinate amount of time on the surface. "Just loafing around," Bill said. Then he shouted, "Look at that!"

One of the humpbacks had raised a black bulbous rostrum above the water.

"It's *inflated*," Bill said, puzzled. It was a peculiar thing for Bill to say. Humpback whales don't inflate their rostrums. They have no means of doing so, and no reason. The whales turned our way, and we saw the dorsal fins characteristic of humpback whales. In fact there were no dorsal fins. We manufactured them in our imaginations, as cleverly as hunters make cows into deer. We had been seeing humpbacks all spring. We expected humpbacks. We saw humpbacks.

The humpback with the inflated rostrum detached itself from the others and came toward us, as if to investigate. That dark, bulbous nose cruised toward us, then, eighty yards away, it disappeared beneath the surface. We were slow getting into the water. The humpback's surface behavior was so odd, so interesting, that we didn't want to miss any of it. We sat frozen, like Greek sailors after a siren song. Suddenly the black dome resurfaced, glistening, ten feet from the boat. The whale braked easily, turning away in a gentle swirl of water.

"*That's a sperm whale,*" said Bill. In one motion he pushed his mask into place and rolled over the side.

For an instant I believed him, but by the time I had

adjusted my mask and followed him, I had changed my mind. I knew that divers can't get this close to sperm whales. Bill was kidding me now, or mistaken.

Underwater I saw an enormous whale. It was so close that Bill's torso and head fit inside the silhouette. The whale filled up half the ocean. I remember thinking, *So that's how a humpback looks underwater,* then realizing instantaneously that this was no humpback. It was a sperm whale, all right, and there were two of them, a big one near us and a smaller whale behind. They were stockier and more powerful than in any sperm-whale picture I had seen. They were beautiful. I glimpsed the white of the underslung jaw and the shallowly serrate crest running down the spine. The crest ended in a high point, and it was this that our imaginations had transformed into a dorsal fin. The two whales were moving away without real haste, but they were so fast, in their effortless way, that in five seconds they were gone.

Back in the boat, our voices shook with adrenalin. I can't remember what we said at first, but Chris started up the twin Mercuries and we headed after the whales. "Did you get the picture?" I asked Bill. He thought he had, but he wasn't sure. He'd had no time to do anything but pull the trigger.

"We've got to do this," he said, as we flanked the whales and motored ahead. "We've got to do this. We've just got to do this." I wasn't sure what he meant. Was it simply that we had to make the best of this opportunity? Or did he mean that we had to get photographs in spite of the danger?

"Say, what about these whales?" asked Chris.

"That's right," I said. "These are *sperm* whales. That's a big toothed whale."

It was a sperm whale, after all, that had carried Ahab to his grave. It was sperm whales, jaws agape, that splintered whaleboats in those old lithographs and sent the sailors in parabolas through the air. No less an authority than Baron Cuvier himself, the great rationalist who once decried "that heated imagination which leads some enthusiasts to see nothing in nature but miracles and monsters," had written, of the sperm whale, "The terrible arms, the powerful and numerous teeth with which nature has provided the cachalot, render it a terrific adversary to all the inhabitants of the deep, even to those which are most dangerous to others; such as the phocae, the balaenopterae, the dolphin, and the shark. So terrified are all these animals at the sight of the cachalot, that they hurry to conceal themselves from him in the sands or mud, and often in the precipitancy of their flight, dash themselves against the rocks with such violence as to cause instantaneous death."

From the stomachs of sperm whales, scientists have recovered skates, snappers, sardines, seals, scorpaenids, sharks, sponges, spiny lobsters, lampreys, pike, angler fish, rock cod, ragfish, rattails, crayfish, crabs, jellyfish, tunicates, rocks, sand, glass buoys, gorgonians, coral, coconuts, wood, apples, fish line, hooks, shoes, baling wire, plastic bags. A creature that gorged on gorgonians and baling wire might just as easily gorge on Billy and Chris. An animal that could catch and swallow a ten-foot blue shark—and sperm whales have done so—would have no trouble catching and downing me. I had an intuition that I was safe with these whales, but it was a shaky intuition. We had no idea what the risks were, for as far as we knew, nobody had tried this before. None of us wanted to stop. It was, I remember thinking, like a sudden invitation to join an expedition to Mars. We had a chance to see things other men haven't. Better to slide like Jonah down the gullet than to kick yourself the rest of your life.

We followed the sperm whales all morning, but they never let us close. Again and again we cut the outboards and waited ahead of them, but they always altered course. "They know right where we are," said Bill, watching the serrate backs turn aside once more. "They have all the equipment."

There were five to ten whales, at least one calf among them. They swam in a tight group, except for the large animal that had first investigated us. The big whale, an outrider, often positioned itself between us and the others. This was, I learned later, normal behavior in bull sperm whales protecting their families.

We tried swimming far off from the Boston whaler, in hopes that the whales, in turning to avoid the boat, would come toward us. We waited, sculling in place, trying to make no noise. The underwater blue seemed as close and featureless as that dark that comes when you shut your eyes. Everything we thought we saw there was imaginary. No shape of whale appeared.

I looked toward Bill and caught his eye. Looking back, he cupped his hand to his ear, symbolically. I realized then that we had been hearing something. Out of the blue came an insistent, slow, evenly spaced *tok tok tok*. It was the sperm whale sonar. It was as riveting as any humpback's song. The signal came from one of the biggest and most penetrating of cetacean instruments. It was the ratchet noise of the kikos, but played much slower and deeper, as one would expect from a creature hundreds of times larger. It charged the blue with mystery as the blue had never been charged before. The depths under you become something else again, when it's a sperm whale that might rise out of them. We observed nothing in the blue, yet, *tok tok tok tok,* we were being observed.

Late in the morning the whales headed seaward, and we gave up on them.

"That's the first whale I've ever seen good underwater," I said, as we watched them go.

Bill gave me a look. He shook his head at my beginner's luck. My first whale, and it was a sperm whale.

I was troubled, though, that I couldn't remember the whale better. My recollection was blurry. When I mentioned this, Bill concurred. "I can't remember," he said, "having a recollection that's any fuzzier." He could recall the deep morning blue of the water, and the blackness and smoothness of the whales, but he was vague about detail. I decided that the problem was in our expectation of humpback. There had been a brief war between the expected outlines and the real ones, and it had smeared the whales in our memories. It was as if the whales possessed a mystifying aura. It was as if they had sent out some kind of scrambling signal to excise their images sonically, preserving some secret.

"I want to see them one more time," I said, aloud. To myself I swore an oath that, given another chance, I would see them more clearly.

"You never see enough," Bill replied. "It's always like that. It's like when you were a kid and you saw your first tit. You can't look enough."

It was famine or feast with us. Now that our bad luck had changed, things kept getting better.

The day after the sperm whales, as we left Keauhou Harbor in the morning, I thought I saw a blow to the northwest. We turned that way, and immediately I began to lose confidence. It was a gray, breezy day, and the sea was running with small whitecaps. I began to think that a whitecap was all I'd seen. I told Chris tentatively I guessed I was wrong. Then I told him positively. He had just swerved back on course when we saw a spout for sure, nearer now. "It's not a porpoise blow," Bill said. It was too big for that. We saw another blow, then another. "It's not a sperm whale," said Bill. "I wonder what the hell it is." We realized, after yesterday's sperm whale, that this whale could be anything.

Drawing abreast of the school, we paced it for a while, looking down on dorsal fins unlike anything we had seen in Hawaii. They were big and rather falcate, with odd, rounded tips. Some of the fins were much bigger than

Kiko calf leaping to dislodge remora

others. The dorsals, and the blunt heads that sometimes broke the surface, made us think these were pilot whales, or perhaps pygmy killer whales, a rare species that frequents Hawaiian waters. The whales did not seem bothered by us. They held to the same course, and it was easy to line up in front of them. We jumped in the water and waited, spy-hopping several times to make sure we were still on line. Onward came the big fins, so we sank underwater.

The ocean that day was the blue I liked best. Little light was penetrating the clouds, and still less penetrated the surface of the sea. The blue in those conditions was dim yet somehow vibrant. The new whales took shape in that color and came out of it toward us. For me it was like seeing my first kiko all over again. Two whales passed to one side of us, and several passed below. They were built on the dolphin plan, clearly, but were blunt-nosed and much bigger than *Stenella* or *Steno.* Had it not been for the sperm whales yesterday, these whales would have looked gigantic. I had never seen a pilot whale in the flesh, but these looked like the pilot whales in pictures. One whale, as it ascended to breathe, emitted a voluble, birdy snatch of song. The top of its head disappeared for a moment above the surface as the whale blew, then the great back curved down again, the blowhole trailing a line of bubbles.

When they had passed, we swam to the boat and clambered in. Chris started up the outboards and spun the wheel. As we sped after the whales, we began comparing notes.

The three of us had a way of collectively filling in the detail of our cetaceans. We all seemed to notice different things. Just now, Bill and Chris both had been struck by the tiny, white, sharky eye of this new whale. I hadn't noticed that, but I had seen the crescentic slit of the closed blowhole as a whale passed beneath. Next time Bill and Chris would look for that, and I would look for the sharky eye.

"Sun!" pleaded Bill, gazing skyward. For photography

The dolphin's reservoir of survival craft, which once lay in such land adaptations as fleetness and the ability to sort out the faintest hint of a telltale odor from vastly stronger smells, became blunted. New priorities of danger had to be classified and understood from the swelling and diminishing shoals of sound coming from far beyond the limits of vision. Our animal had to learn which sounds told only of the ordinary thermal layering in the sea that scattered and jumbled sounds like light streaming through wavy glass, and which ones told a more relevant story.

· · ·

he needed more light underwater. There were promising rents in the clouds, but the sun was not above any of them. "Come on, sun," he prayed. "Come on, sun."

We caught up with the fins again. This time, we saw two truly enormous dorsals among the others.

"What's the word for it, when one sex is larger than the other?" Bill asked.

We knew the word perfectly well, but no one could think of it. "Polyandry," I said. "Polygamy. Androgeny. Fellatio."

"Dimorphism!" Bill shouted.

We agreed that this species, whatever it was, demonstrated strong sexual dimorphism. We lined up on the whales and watched them come.

"These sure are straight-line dolphins," I said.

"They sure are," said Bill.

In their navigation, these new whales had a singleness of purpose that the kikos lacked. They were headed straight toward Maui as if that's where they intended to go.

"I bet we don't see as much this time," I predicted, as we poised to enter the water again. I had noticed, on previous days, that a school's first pass, when the dolphins were their most curious about us, was usually the best. This time I was wrong. Moments after my prophecy, underwater behind Bill, I saw the ocean brighten suddenly, as if someone had flipped a switch. The sun, in answer to Bill's prayer, had come out in the universe above. Toward us came a mother and calf, their backs and flanks veined with sunlight. The calf rolled over and began to nurse. The mother was indifferent to us. Making a slight course correction so as not to hit Bill, she passed serenely by, her calf nursing all the way. Bill made a fluid turn and followed, kicking lazily, not wanting to frighten her, his motor-drive firing away. The calf was still nursing as the two whales disappeared, and the last thing we saw of them was the white of the calf's belly, canted up toward the surface. Bill looked at me, his eyes wide in disbelief. He would have howled with happiness, I think, except that it might have alarmed a second wave of whales, which in a moment would be here. "I was watching it all through the viewfinder," he wrote later in his journal, "and as the mother and calf passed beneath and a little off to the side they were full frame horizontal and it was an incredible lovely sight."

We stayed with the whales nearly five hours, jumping into the water a dozen times. With each dive we fleshed out the whales out a bit more. We grew familiar with the white, impacted eye; the subtle, dark cape in the shape of an hourglass atop the head and dorsum; the shallow, craterlike depressions of healed cookie-cutter wounds; the long, white, double and triple scratch lines where the whales had relieved their itches; the insignificant beak on the underside of the blunt head; the strange, pursed smile, fixed permanently in place; the communication, which reminded Bill of a beluga's canary warbling. It was a big, blunt, powerful dolphin. The caudal peduncle, the hump directly forward of the flukes, seemed stuffed tight with muscle, like the hump of a bull. I wondered about the niche of this superdolphin, here in the territory of the kikos. It seemed likely that it hunted deeper than kikos. The kikos were said to feed out here in the daytime; perhaps these big dolphins fed at night. They seemed to be at rest now, moving at an easy pace in one direction, never diving.

Bill decided they were not pilot whales. They were like the pilots he knew from southern California, but shorter,

Spotted dolphin, Hawaii

It learned to feel nuances of pressure in the passing water. It eventually was able to adjust
effortlessly to the great changing weight of water as it dove, and its body became terete
and delicately balanced in the yielding fluid. Perhaps it also learned to taste its world, for
its nostrils proved of little use at sea. Perhaps the porpoise came to understand the
molecular hints that flowed past its tongue and that might tell in acridity that a great shark
had just passed.

—KENNETH NORRIS

Spotted dolphins, Hawaii

Let us try for a moment to enter the dolphin's kingdom and the dolphin's body, retaining, at the same time, our human intelligence. In this imaginative act, it may be possible to divest ourselves of certain human preconceptions about our kind of intelligence and at the same time to see more clearly why mind, even advanced mind, may have manifestations other than the tools and railroad tracks and laboratories that we regard as evidence of intellect. If we are particularly adept in escaping from our own bodies, we may even learn to discount a little the kind of world of rockets and death that our type of busy human curiosity, linked to a hand noted for its ability to open assorted Pandora's boxes, has succeeded in foisting upon the world as a symbol of universal intelligence.

We have now sacrificed, in our imagination, or hands for flippers and our familiar land environment for the ocean. We will go down into the deep waters as naked of possessions as when we entered life itself. We will take with us one thing alone that exists among porpoises as among men: an ingrained biological gregariousness—a sociality that in our new world will permit us to run in schools.

. . .

with a different color pattern, and with a larger and more falcate dorsal fin. We began to call them pygmy killers. Later we would learn that they were pilot whales after all, but of a race very different from the one in California.

We hauled ourselves out of the water for the last time. The pilot whales continued on their march toward Maui, and we watched them go. Bill pulled off his flippers and studied them, meditatively. They were no longer shiny black, like my new pair, but gray with scratches and abrasions. "These Jetfins have swum with right whales," he said, and he kissed them. "Gray whales." He kissed the rubber again. "Killer whales." Another kiss. "Humpbacks." Kiss. "Narwhals." Kiss. "Minke whales." Kiss. "Sperm whales." Kiss. "And now these guys, pygmy killers, or whatever they are."

Seven days later, after spending our time with kikos, we met pilot whales again. After our week with the man-sized kikos, the dimensions of the pilots were momentarily disconcerting. They came at us as big as attenuated elephants but chirping like an aviary. They dove shallowly to avoid us. Their greater size and length gave them more momentum than the kikos, and on ceasing to swim they could glide much farther. They passed under us locked in motionless formation, dark torpedos in the blue gloaming. The adult animals, as before, did not look up. We were beneath their interest, or above it, technically. They had seen it all already; nothing in the sea surprised them anymore. Their broad backs, and the scars of old episodes, sailed under us without a movement from the flukes, as if a current were running down there. The calves and juveniles were not so jaded. They rolled sideways to look at us, showing the white of their bellies.

In our second dive, one of the whales—it was impossible to tell which—repeated a single note five or six times. It was different from the usual warbling. It sounded like a query that we were supposed to answer. Probably it was something else, a poem or a curse or a grumble—it's foolish to hope for cognates in languages that diverged sixty million years ago. One group, three mothers and three calves, passed to the side, a mobile nursery.

In our third dive, a whale passed with two remoras attached. We saw another with its dorsal fin partly bitten off—a shark? A third whale swam along with its eyes closed—the eye on our side, anyway. My own eyes, tracking that whale, came to Bill and saw that he was studying the water below me. I looked down and saw a juvenile whale the size of a Volkswagen rising belly-up toward me. At one end of the pale belly was the pursed smile, at the other end the genital slit. I remembered Bill's story about the misdirected amorousness of juvenile harp seals. I hoped pilots weren't that way—I did not want to be violated by an

Nursing pilot whale, Hawaii

animal the size of a Volkswagen. The young whale ratcheted me at point-blank range, then sank again.

In our fourth dive, I was at Bill's shoulder underwater when we saw a medium-sized pilot coming for us straighter than any pilot yet had come. All we could see was a dark sphere in the water, and the pilot's scientific name, *Globicephala melaena,* became perfectly apt. The sonar dome detected us, and the whale slowed. In an attempt to see us, or to fill us in acoustically, it slowly nodded its head, which for us meant that a mouth appeared at the lower edge of the globe, migrated toward the top, then migrated back again. The whale interrupted its normal breathing sequence. It stopped short of the surface and, instead of blowing, it sank tailfirst. Vertical in the water, it turned slightly to put an eye on us. It took a good look, then went up quickly for the interrupted breath. It blew, dove, and continued on its way.

The last pilots of this pass disappeared in the blue. We sculled around in slow circles, looking for a straggler. We saw nothing but the familiar three hundred and sixty degrees of blue, and a single remora moving away from us. The remora swam on its side with the odd motion of the species, its oblong sucker toward us. Perhaps it had detached from a pilot whale in hopes of settling on one of us. On coming close, it had not liked the look of us. Bill handed me his camera and sprinted after the remora. He almost overtook it, but it managed to elude his fingers. After twenty yards he gave up, and we returned to the boat.

From deck, we saw that the pilots were making their beeline toward a distant cluster of skiffs. There were seven or eight boats, which meant the fishermen were working kikos. Realizing that there might be a meeting of pilots and kikos, we began to get excited. We kept pace with the pilots, waiting for one or the other of the converging cetacean schools to turn off. Neither did. The big, dark dorsals of the pilots mingled with the small gray dorsals of the kikos. We raced ahead of the confluence of schools

The result is immediately evident and quite clear: No matter how well we communicate with our fellows through the water medium we will never build drowned empires in the coral; we will never inscribe on palace walls the victorious boasts of porpoise kings. We will know only water and the wastes of water beyond the power of man to describe. We will be secret visitors in hidden canyons beneath the mouths of torrential rivers. We will survey in innocent astonishment the flotsam that pours from the veins of continents—dead men, great serpents, giant trees—or perhaps the little toy boat of a child loosed far upstream will come floating past. Bottles with winking green lights will plunge by us into the all-embracing ooze. Meaningless appearances and disappearances will comprise our philosophies. We will hear the earth's heart ticking in its thin granitic shell. Volcanic fires will growl ominously in steam-filled crevices. Vapor, bird cries and sea wrack will compose our memories. We will see death in many forms and, on occasion, the slow majestic fall of battleships through the green light that comes from beyond our domain.

.   .   .

and jumped in. The first time underwater we saw nothing but kikos. We swam to the boat, climbed in, and raced ahead again. This time, after several waves of kikos shot by us underwater, we saw, distantly, a single pilot whale with an escort of fifteen kikos. The kikos cavorted in a tight group around the pilot, like gray dogs harrying a black bear, except that everyone seemed to be having fun. I had not realized, before this direct comparison, how much smaller, paler, and more flexible the kikos were. It was a nice demonstration of the diversity within the dolphin family. The kikos circled the pilot, waving their rostrums, flexing their flukes. Those kikos in front were probably jockeying for position on the larger animal's pressure wave. If a human can read anything at all in the body language of dolphins, then the kikos were in good spirits. They were enjoying this demonstration of their greater maneuverability. The pilot's body English—its body dolphinese—was more difficult to read. I had an intuition, whatever it is worth, that the pilot was enjoying the company of its cousins and this demonstration of its greater bulk and purpose.

Moments later, the two schools pulled apart, continuing on their separate paths.

"Did you get a picture?" I asked Bill, when we reached the side of the boat.

"They were too far away. I got a 'record' shot, anyway. Maybe they can blow it up."

We broke for lunch. As we ate, I studied Bill for evidence of disappointment. We had come so close to getting a picture. He was not saying much—a bad sign, usually. He spooned the black seeds of his papaya overboard, and they drifted down like the roe of some huge sturgeon. He ate the fruit quickly, threw the skin overboard, and watched it sink.

"Plenty no more papaya," he said absent-mindedly, in what was supposed to be pidgin.

Slowly he turned to us, his eyes widening in wild surmise.

"Plenty no more papaya," he repeated. Then again, "Plenty no more papaya," this time making it sound a bit more cheerful and dumb. Chris and I exchanged hopeless glances. A new motto was being born. The line, I had to admit, had inevitability. Bill had stumbled upon something. There was a horrible contagion in these discoveries of his. I mouthed the words silently in my head, then found them rising to my lips. "Plenty no more papaya," I said softly, experimentally. "Plenty no more papaya," I repeated, louder, hating myself. I felt Chris staring at me and I avoided his eyes.

At 9:40 one morning, five miles offshore, we saw a fin we had missed for a while, the dark, sizable dorsal of *Steno*, the rough-toothed dolphin. We jumped in the water and renewed our acquaintance.

In our first two dives that day, we joined what could have been a nuclear family, if dolphins had those—two adults and a calf. We realized now that our first steno, that solitary scout who had greeted us weeks before, was no more scarred and mottled than any grown steno. All adults were that way. The rough-toothed dolphin is a marked-up race. The calf was curious and it looped back to look at us. It swam with a goofy, playful wobble, showing us alternately the white of its belly and the dark of its dorsum. It strayed farther from its mother than kiko calves did, and the mother did not seem to mind.

Kiko calf leaping (again) to dislodge remora

Bill poked his head above the water. "That calf sure had a nice face," he said.

We all liked the stenos. They weren't so desperately gregarious as the kikos and spinners. They seemed to enjoy spending a little time by themselves. In intelligence tests devised by humans, stenos are the brightest of dolphins, whatever that proves. I liked the stenos for their scars, for the harder life the scars suggested. I liked their plain faces. Stenos lack the pronounced bulge in the forehead that most dolphins have. The line from the beak to the top of the head is a smooth, slightly concave curve. I liked the individuality in their markings. The underside of each animal was mottled differently. The patterns were white and circular, like lichen rings on dark, wet stones.

At first today, the stenos were scattered, making it difficult to find more than two together. The third time we dove, however, they seemed to be convening, and Bill noticed fish scales in the water. We dove a fourth time, and at last saw a group underwater. They swam slowly toward us. Held crosswise in the mouth of one, unexpected, silvery, impossible, was a twenty-pound *mahi mahi*. I looked at Bill to see if he'd seen His gaze was fixed on the fish.

The mahi mahi, or dolphinfish, or *dorado*, is one of the fastest swimmers in the ocean, designed to chase down flying fish. In the previous weeks we had trolled for mahi mahi whenever we passed the floating objects they like to hang under. We had seen them streak like bullets for the lure, half out of the ocean, water planing from their blunt heads. How could a dolphin catch a fish like that? Maybe, I thought, they hadn't caught it. Maybe the fish had died, and the dolphin simply had found it. The steno was just carrying it along, like a dog with a stick. I convinced myself the fish was just a plaything. Then the dolphin shifted it to the corner of the mouth and chewed.

There were ten dolphins. They were swimming close together, moving so slowly that we could almost pace them in our Jetfins. They were directly below us now, about sixty feet down. We saw the keeper of the fish drop it. It drifted end-over-end into the path of another dolphin, which took it without breaking stride. The new dolphin chewed once, then it just held the fish by the head. A third dolphin came up slowly on the shoulder of the second and closed its jaws on the tail, at which the second released it. Then the original dolphin took it again.

Over all that region of wondrous beauty we will exercise no more control than the simplest mollusc. Even the octopus with flexible arms will build little shelters that we cannot imitate. Without hands we will have only the freedom to follow the untrammeled sea winds across the planet.

. . .

Bill's head was gone above the surface, which meant he wanted to talk. I surfaced myself.

"*Can you believe this?*" he yelled.

"That's a mahi mahi!" I yelled back. "How did those guys catch a mahi mahi?"

The dolphins were pulling away from us, so Bill signaled Chris to bring the boat over. At the whine of the outboards, the dolphins dove in formation. It was a steep, slow, unworried dive. Thirty-five feet down, their flukes stopped working. The dolphins froze, like a frame jammed in the projector. All ten stenos were in identical attitudes of pitch and yaw, the flukes of all pointed directly at the surface. The group were just shadows now, except for the mahi mahi, which glinted silver in the filtered light. They coasted—ghosted—down toward the bottom of the sea, as if this were a suicide pact. The last we saw of them was the white flesh of the mahi mahi, progressing eerily, as if by a fitful locomotion of its own.

Six days later we met stenos again, and again they had a mahi mahi. This time we saw the fish before we got in the water. It was clamped in the beak of a steno as the dolphin broke the surface to blow. In its instant above the water, the fish shimmered gold and green and electric blue. We knew that a mahi mahi's iridescendence fades within a minute or two of its death. This one must have been freshly caught.

Seeing this second fish was as startling, nearly, as seeing the first. The second proved the first was no fluke. It suggested that the rough-toothed dolphin specialized in mahi mahi, one of the ocean's supreme sprinters. How did they do it?

I reviewed the little I knew about mahi mahi. They ate flying fish. They were not very bright. (We had watched them swim in a group around a hooked compatriot, waiting their turn to take the lure, and once we had caught three that way.) They liked to hang underneath floating objects. *Floating objects.* Was it possible that one steno lay at the surface, a decoy, its blowhole above the water, imitating a floating log? That still left the problem of chasing down the fish. To do that, stenos used teamwork, surely.

Maybe the mahi mahi was like a human sprinter, good for bursts of speed, but poor at endurance. Maybe the dolphins ran it down in relays. The fish was the speeder. The dolphins were the highway patrolmen, radio equipped, waiting at intervals down the road. Bill had made an observation that fit in with that: the only time we saw stenos close together, he pointed out, was when they had succeeded in catching a fish: the rest of the time they were widely scattered.

When we joined the stenos underwater, their behavior was the same as on the earlier day. Again they swam very slowly and close together. Again a single animal seemed keeper of the fish. (Today the keeper was an easy dolphin to distinguish, because it was very mottled on its underside and flanks.) The keeper chewed from time to time, using for leverage a swimming motion, a shallow, rapid undulation that traveled from flukes to head. It did not resist when others moved up on its shoulder to pull a piece off, and sometimes it gave up the fish entirely. The manners of the school were impeccable. When a white piece of fish shook loose, one of the keeper's wingmen turned back for it, slowly and politely, not trying to beat anyone to it. Once the keeper dropped the fish, and it drifted up toward us. No one tried to steal it. The keeper turned a slow backward somersault and seized it again.

We stuck our heads above the water for a conversation. It was, Bill said, their etiquette that distinguished these dolphins from everything else in the sea. "Can you imagine, say, *sharks* with something like that?" he asked.

Was the keeper, I wondered, the dominant dolphin in the tribe, or was it just the catcher of the fish? Or both? Maybe for the duration of the meal, the catcher was king. Maybe the stenos' subsistence society was like human subsistence societies; the successful hunter gets the best cuts, but finds his real reward in sharing with the group.

The fish was rapidly diminishing. In successive dives, we noticed less and less of it. In our last dive, there was hardly any fish left at all, and before we could enter the water again, the dolphins had dispersed once more.

Bill never got close enough for a good picture. He had tried using the pony tank to get deep, where the dolphins did most of their eating, but his bubbles had spooked them. We had no time to lament this, for now, from the southwest, came a big school of kikos. They were swimming faster than any kikos we had ever seen. They made a front a half mile across, ripping along so fast that twenty at a time were entirely airborne. Gangs of shearwaters hunted the school's leading edge, chasing the surface fish that the kikos were flushing like quail. We saw a frigate bird, a black speck sailing just under the indigo stratosphere on fixed wings. We lost track of it; then, scarcely a minute later, we saw it low on the water chasing a flying fish. It is impossible, of course, for a bird with a seven-foot wingspan to trim quickly enough to catch a flying fish, and inevitably the frigate missed. We were amused, but admired the frigate's spirit. As we smiled, a dolphin chased another flying fish out of the water, and the frigate took the fish on the wing.

Bill was stunned. "I can't believe we're seeing this," he said. "I can't believe that we're seeing this."

We jumped into the water, but the dolphins were by us so quickly that Bill lacked time to level his camera. They came through so fast they scarcely had time to glance at us, and no time at all to threaten. Not one broke stride. I picked one calf and timed it. It scuttled through my field of view, which must have extended at least a hundred feet in either direction, in about eight seconds.

We returned to the boat and hurried after the dolphins.

The exuberance of the speed-swimming had spread first among the members of the school, then to the birds, and finally to us. As we chased after, I saw the most beautiful leap I had ever seen; no acrobatics, nothing fancy, just a broadjump of incredible height and distance. For a moment it took my wind away. Then we watched two dolphins race up from behind us, on the port side. They surfed for a moment on our wake, then accelerated, swimming with perfect synchrony, matching each other stride for stride. They passed under us so quickly we just had time to shift attention to starboard, and there they leapt, emerging as mirror images, just missing the boat. They returned in a double arc, both beaks striking the water at precisely the same instant. I saw Chris shake his head with emotion. "How can they do that?" he asked. "How can they be synchronized like that?"

Once more the kikos showed us something new. Before, these flurries of speed had never lasted long. Today we kept telling one another that they couldn't keep this up much longer. Half an hour later they were still going strong. We had to stop. They were flying too fast for photography. We watched as they lathered the water white all the way to the horizon, then beyond, disappearing over the curve of the Earth.

The two months on the water had transformed us. We were burned as brown as our respective ancestries permitted. Bill's hair and mine was bleached blond-white. Chris's lips were cracking. Bill's dark-blue T-shirt retained its original color only where the shoulder straps of his Farmer Johns protected it; the rest had faded nearly white. We were acclimatized. We still suffered from the conditions we called Snorkel Mouth and Wetsuit Ass, but these were in remission. Snorkel Mouth was a reaction to the plastic of the snorkel mouthpiece, compounded by the

Spotted dolphins, Hawaii

irritation of salt water, and it felt like cold sores. We winced every time we had to stretch our lips around the mouthpiece. Wetsuit Ass was a rash of bumps from the friction of our wetsuits bouncing against the boat seats. There was nothing to be done about either malady, and we had been afflicted so long we scarcely noticed, anyway.

There were rough days when the Boston whaler, planing over the sea, slapped down hard, jarring us to the bone. It was like being punched; you saw red for an instant and looked for somebody to punch back, but there was no one aboard but friends. We *were* friends, mostly, though the days were hot and long and sometimes argumentative.

I remember the salt that granulated our forearms, a precipitate of the spray. The same white patterns formed every day. I remember blurry days underwater, the ocean gauzy with its gelatinous disks, spheres, and filaments, as if we had been injected somehow into a macrocosmic bloodstream full of white cells and platelets. On those days we saw all our dolphins through a diatomaceous curtain. I remember other days, the water so clear, so empty of organisms, that the dolphins seemed to be flying through air, except for the wave-patterned sunlight that danced along the backs of those animals closest to the surface. I remember the big cane spider that stowed away in the throttle of the Boston whaler, accompanying us seaward for two days in a row. The spider was the same pale red as the volcanic dust that powdered the cane fields. We were sorry when, on peering into the throttle the third morning, we saw that our mascot, weary of sailing, had jumped ship in the night. I remember the squid we stole from a shearwater. The squid, a big one, had drifted up half eaten in the wake of a kiko school, and the shearwater had had the meat all to itself until we robbed it, jamming head and tentacles into the ice chest to eat later ourselves. I remember entire days in which Bill and Chris communicated only in their joke CB language, and how tired I got of that. I remember the blue shark we saw under a floating can. The can was rusted. The shark was beautiful, with the sharp nose and long pectoral fins of its species. The shark moved off reluctantly as we drew alongside the can. When we pulled away, the shark returned. The shark and the can resumed their thing together, just the two of them, alone in that blue Sahara.

I remember the questions we asked ourselves. Why did kikos have more remoras than spinners did? Why were rough-toothed dolphins so scratched up? Did pilot whales regularly circumnavigate the island of Hawaii, as they seemed to, and if so, why? What went on out here, in the depths, at night? I remember realizing, one day, that the kikos traveled in homogenous groups. That tendency could not have been more obvious, yet we had to see it dozens of times before we really marked it. There were gangs of juveniles swimming along in one another's company—medium-sized animals whose flanks were as yet unspotted, whose beaks were not yet white-tipped. And there were squads of grown males, big animals with white-spotted sides that traveled boldly and fast behind the white dots of rank on their noses. It was the squads of males that veered close to ratchet and threaten us, we realized, never the younger animals. Another day I realized that I could see, almost, the beam of clicks emanating from the white dot. I could predict at exactly what point, in the swing of a beak toward me, I would begin hearing the ratchet noise. As the beak came on target, the clicks crescendoed, as if the dolphin were a Geiger counter and I the radioactive substance. The beam was narrower than I would have guessed; the beak had to point to within three or four degrees of me to sound me out. The beam was conical, it seemed, beginning small and spreading outward, so that a near dolphin had to point more directly at me than a dolphin in the middle distance did. At long distance, the resolution of the dolphin's acoustic picture seemed to fall off, so that far dolphins again had to point straight at me, or so I thought. I remember nights on the water, the sky west of us glowing with zodiacal light, the sea in our wake bioluminescent. I remember the daytime, and how perfectly silent the ocean became when, out beyond sight and sound of the surf, the wind dropped.

Of the three of us, Bill best liked the elevation of the console, our crow's nest, and he spent the most time up there. On spotting dolphins, he slapped the painter like reins on the console, urging the boat on, and he gave a cowboy whoop. He whipped off his red sun-brim and waved it wildly in the air. Sometimes there were no dolphins, but Bill slapped the reins, whooped, and waved the brim anyway, as if to raise a school by sympathetic magic.

Ashore one day, reading *Sports Illustrated,* Bill learned that baseball season was about to begin on the mainland. Baseball is the one sport he ever cared anything about. Suddenly he missed it. On opening day, in the middle of the blue water, thousands of miles from the nearest ballpark, Bill, standing on the console, broke tentatively into song. "Take me out to the ball game, take me out to the park . . . His spirit and volume grew. ". . . so it's root toot toot for the home team, if we don't win it's a shame . . ." He finished with great feeling, ripping off his sun-brim and gesturing operatically with it. We liked the performance so much that the song became our anthem. We sang it unaccompanied until Chris brought his harmonica one day. From then on we had music.

One gray day, we saw a strange blow to the northwest. Chris spun the wheel and we headed there; he standing at the helm, I at his shoulder, Billy up on his crow's nest, where he gripped the painter, his knees bent slightly to take the shock of the waves. We gazed ahead. "It's not a dolphin," Billy said. "It's not a humpback. I wonder what the hell this is."

He held his red sun-brim in his hand, extended a bit for balance. In a moment he might wave it in the air, then give his cowboy yell and slap the reins on the deck. For now the red sun-brim remained poised. Billy's eyes were rapt on the horizon.

I realized that this, for me, was the moment. Ahead, on the dark, impenetrable surface of the sea, was some unidentified cetacean. It blew again. One day, that blow had belonged to Cuvier's beaked whale. I had not known, before meeting Cuvier's whale, that such an animal existed. Another day the spout had belonged to a sperm whale, another day to *Steno bredanensis,* another to *Globicephala malaena.* Today the creature ahead of us could be anything. I realized there was no place I would rather be, that I could do this happily every day for the rest of my natural life.

We closed in on the unknown whale.

*The whales turn and glisten, plunge
and sound and rise again,
Hanging over subtly darkening deeps
Flowing like breathing planets
in the sparkling whorls of
living light.*
—GARY SNYDER

In the still air of the afternoon the little sounds are few and far between, like the whisperings of a desert land, though the sea below is all aquiver with subdued noise—the ultrasounds of a thousand whales communicating with one another and holding their group together by invisible cords.

—VICTOR SCHEFFER

Rough-toothed dolphins with mahi mahi, Hawaii

Moving through a dim, dark, cool, watery world of its own, the whale is timeless and ancient; part of our common heritage and yet remote, awful, prowling the ocean floor a half-mile down, under the guidance of powers and senses we are only beginning to grasp.
—VICTOR SCHEFFER

Sperm whales, Hawaii

Gray whale and kelp, California

What is it in our nature that propels us to continue to hunt initiated in earlier times?
Are we like some lethal mechanical toy that will not wind down until the last bomb
explodes in the last whale's side? What is it that makes so small a thing of eliminating
in our lifetime the oceanic role of the largest creature that has lived on our planet?
What is it that kills the goose that lays the golden egg? It is already too late? Is our own
obituary scrawled in the fates of the bowhead and right whale, the blue and the humpback?
—SCOTT McVAY

Humpback whale at sunset, Newfoundland

Blue whale, Newfoundland

In a world older and more complete than ours they move finished and complete, gifted with extensions of the senses we have lost or never attained, living by voices we shall never hear. They are not brethren, they are not underlings; they are other nations, caught with ourselves in the net of life and time, fellow prisoners of the splendor and travail of the earth.
—HENRY BESTON

Humpback whale and calf, Hawaii

Acknowledgments

THIS BOOK would not exist without the understanding and support of Robert Gilka of the *National Geographic*. On occasion I have returned from a marine-mammal assignment without a single photograph to show the editors. It has been Bob Gilka's awareness of the difficulties in this kind of photography, and his sense of its value, that have, over the years, greatly helped this endeavor. To him I owe a special thanks.

I am grateful to the *National Geographic* for its support and to the following for their help over the years: Gilbert M. Grosvenor, Sam Matthews, W. Allan Royce, Robert S. Patton, Ann Dirks Kobor, and Thelma Altemus; to the National Science Foundation and its Division of Polar Programs; to Jane Kinne and Suzanne Goldstein of Photo Researchers; and to Philip M. Smith, Paul Dayton, Gerald Kooyman, Kenneth Norris, Roger Payne, Steve Leatherwood, Ed Mitchell, Camille Goebel, Joe MacInnis, Jack Skeffington, Steve Sieffert, Ken Balcomb, Chris Newbert, and Andrew MacFarlane, who in large ways and small assisted me in making these photographs.

To Bora Merdsoy, Chuck Nicklin, and Ken Brower I owe much. They have joined me in this quest and have lived with the moments, both high and low, that reside in such an adventure.

A dozen years ago I found myself inside a book, *On the Loose* by Terry and Renny Russell, published by David Brower and the Sierra Club. The words addressed my every thought and helped me through a period when I was living the antithesis of a life "on the loose." That book and all the others David Brower has produced for Sierra Club and Friends of the Earth have revealed how splendid a place our planet is and instilled in me a sense of wonder and reverence for its natural gifts. I am honored that he found this work worthy enough to nurture along and eventually publish.

And to Kate, who showed her silkie friend the heart, I owe all. This book is for her.   —W.R.C.

I am grateful to Bill Curtsinger for holding still for this portrait. Like him, I am grateful to David Brower and my debt is somewhat older—first for my paternity, second for exposing my emulsion early to wild places, and third for inventing a book format large enough to accommodate Bill Curtsinger's whales.
                                                          —K.B.

To Keep the World Safe for Cetaceans

Friends of the Earth in the United States, and independent sister organizations of the same name in twenty other countries, advocate the public's interest—especially the public of the future—in rational use of the environment, in building greater respect for the earth and its living diversity.

Publishing is an important part of the international program and helps sustain it. In addition to the titles published in this series, The Earth's Wild Places (see verso of front endpaper), Friends of the Earth (U.S.), its associate, Earth Island Ltd., and its sister organizations have published books on environmental subjects, including many on the subject for energy, the too enterprising search for which constitutes perhaps the major environmental threat. Most are written by or contributed to by Amory Lovins: *Eryri, the Mountains of Longing; Only One Earth: The Stockholm Conference; Openpit Mining; World Energy Strategies; Nonnuclear Futures; Soft Energy Paths: Toward a Durable Peace; Progress As If Survival Mattered; Sun! A Handbook for the Solar Decade; The Energy Controversy: Soft Path Questions and Answers; New England's White Mountains: At Home in the Wild.*

Membership in FOE in the U.S. ($25 per year) is not tax-deductible; it supports substantial grass-roots lobbying. The FOE Foundation helps finance parts of the program that are tax-deductible (research, education, litigation). Members receive the award-winning periodical, *Not Man Apart*, benefit from generous discounts on FOE's books and the *ECO* published at conferences of international environmental importance, and sustain an extraordinary world-wide effort that can make a difference.

The book is set in Centaur and Arrighi by Mackenzie-Harris Corporation, San Francisco. Separations, lithography, binding and understanding beyond the call of duty are by Arnoldo Mondadori Editore, Verona, Italy, using coated and matte paper by Cartiera Celdit and Bamberger Kaliko Fabrik. The layout is by Kenneth Brower. The design is by David Brower.

Main office: FOE, 124 Spear St., San Francisco, CA 94105.

Kate P. Mahoney

MARINE MAMMAL CONSERVATION GROUPS

The American Cetacean Society, National Headquarters, P.O. Box 4416, San Pedro, CA 90731

Animal Protection Institute, P.O. Box 22505, Sacramento, CA 95822

Animal Welfare Institute, P.O. Box 3650, Washington, D.C. 20007

California Marine Mammal Center, Marin Headlands Ranger Station, Fort Cronkhite, CA 94965

Center for Action on Endangered Species, 175 West Main Street, Ayer, MA 01432

The Connecticut Cetacean Society, 190 Stillwold Drive, Wethersfield, CT 06109

The Cousteau Society, 777 Third Avenue, New York, NY 10017

Defenders of Wildlife, 1233 19th St. N.W., Washington, D.C. 20036

Food and Agriculture Organization/Advisory Committee on Marine Resources, Via delle Terme di Caracalle, Roma 00100, Italy

Friends of the Earth—U.S., 124 Spear Street, San Francisco, CA 94105

Friends of the Earth—U.K., 9 Poland St., London, W1V 3DG, England

Friends of the Earth—France, 14 Bis, Rue de L'Arbalete, 75005, Paris, France

Friends of the Earth—Australia, 232 Castlereagh St., Sydney, 2000, Australia

Friends of the Earth—Canada, 54-53 Queen St., Ottawa, K1P 5C5, Canada

Friends of the Earth—New Zealand, Box 39-065, Auckland West, New Zealand

Fund for Animals, 140 West 57th Street, New York, NY 10019

General Whale, P.O. Box Save the Whale, Alameda, CA 94501

Greenpeace Foundation, 2108 West 4th Avenue, Vancouver, B.C., Canada V6K 1N6

Greenpeace, Off Blackfriars Road, London SE1 8DP, England

Greenpeace, Private Bag, Wellesley St., Auckland, New Zealand

Greenpeace, Building 240, Fort Mason, San Francisco, CA 94123

Humane Society of the U.S., 2100 L Street N.W., Washington, D.C. 20037

IUCN, 1110 Morges, Switzerland

Marine Action Centre, The Bath House, Gwydin St., Cambridge, England

Monitor International, 19102 Roman Way, Gathersburg, Maryland 20760

National Audubon Society, 950 Third Avenue, New York, NY 10022

National Wildlife Federation, 1412 16th St. N.W., Washington, D.C. 20036

Oceanic Society, 240 Fort Maston, San Francisco, CA 94123

Orca Society, University of Washington DB-10, Seattle, WA 98105

Project Jonah—U.S., 41 Nevada St., San Francisco, CA 94110

Project Jonah—Australia, 399 Pitt St., Sydney 2000, Australia

Project Jonah—New Zealand, P.O. Box 42-071, Orakei, Auckland, New Zealand

Rare Animal Relief Effort, c/o National Audubon Society

Sierra Club, 530 Bush St., San Francisco, CA 94108

The Whale Center, 3929 Piedmont Ave., Oakland, CA 94611

The Whale Fund, New York Zoological Society, Bronx Zoo, Bronx, NY 10460

The Whale Protection Fund, 1925 K Street, Washington, D.C. 20006

The Wilderness Society, 1901 Pennsylvania Ave. N.W., Washington, D.C. 20006

Wildlife Society, Suite 611, 7101 Wisconsin Avenue, Washington, D.C. 20016

World Wildlife International, Morges, Switzerland

World Wildlife Fund—U.S., 1601 Connecticut Avenue N.W., Washington, D.C. 20009